Student's Glossary of Literary Terms

Student's Glossary of Literary Terms

Erarbeitet von der Verlagsredaktion:
Neil Porter, Dr. Annelore Naumann-Schütze, Allen Woppert
Assistenz: Rolf Wiesemes

German-English Index von
Dr. James Fanning, Greifswald

Für beratende Mitwirkung danken wir
Prof. Dr. Albert Reiner Glaap, Düsseldorf
Dr. Heinz Antor, Würzburg
Dr. James Fanning, Greifswald

Illustration:
Steven Garner

Technische Umsetzung:
Matthias Fuchs

www.cornelsen.de

1. Auflage, 7. Druck 2006

Alle Drucke dieser Auflage sind inhaltlich unverändert
und können im Unterricht nebeneinander verwendet werden.

© 1992 Cornelsen Verlag, Berlin

Druck: Druckhaus Berlin-Mitte

ISBN-13: 978-3-464-02239-9
ISBN-10:   3-464-02239-0

 Inhalt gedruckt auf säurefreiem Papier,
umweltschonend hergestellt aus chlorfrei gebleichten Faserstoffen.

CONTENTS

Using the Glossary

This glossary of literary terms is designed to help students understand the meaning of terms which are often used when discussing literature. The explanations have been written for students of English who regularly work with English literary texts. The pronunciation of the terms has been provided so that the students will have no difficulty using the terms in classroom discussions. English and American forms of spelling and pronunciation have been given equal consideration.

Cross-references, printed in *italics*, are to be found throughout the work, so that students will be able to understand the differences between various terms and to find other related terms that may be of use in their studies. Titles of books, plays and long poems are printed in SMALL CAPITALS. Where possible, publication dates of the works quoted in the glossary have been supplied.

At the back of the book is a **List of Literary Terms in Wordfields**, which is intended to give the students easier access to important terms they might need when discussing a particular genre or work of literature. Not all the terms in the glossary are listed, since many cannot easily be categorized.

The **German-English Index** is intended for German students who know a term in German and wish to find its equivalent or near equivalent in English.

Abbreviations and symbols

adj.	adjective
ca.	circa; approximately
cf.	confer; compare
e.g.	exempli gratia; for example
etc.	et cetera; and so on
i.e.	id est
Lat.	Latin
n.	noun
pl.	plural
v.	verb
☆	American spelling/pronunciation follows

A

abstract ['æbstrækt] (n.): cf. *summary.*

accumulation [ə,kjuːmjʊ'leɪʃn] (n.): a stylistic device characterized by the piling up of similar words or phrases within a few lines; it serves to emphasize a *description* or impression.
Examples: "Fancy an *old, stumpy, short, vulgar,* and *very dirty* man, in *old* clothes and *shabby old* gaiters"
(William Thackeray, VANITY FAIR; 1847–48)
"And if a young woman has *beauty, birth, breeding, wit, sense, manners* and *modesty*, and all of these to an extreme, yet if she has not money, she's nobody."
(Daniel Defoe, MOLL FLANDERS; 1722)

acrostic [ə'krɒstɪk ☆ -'krɑːst-] (n.): a *poem* in which the first letters of each *line* make a word or verbal pattern when read downwards. The word usually refers to the *theme* of the poem. An acrostic may also be found in *prose* when the first letters of each paragraph form a word.
Example: "*L*ook at that girl
*O*h! My heart is
*V*ery shaky.
*E*verybody needs love."
(Nhoeung Soth, "Love"; ca. 1980)

act [ækt] (n.): the major division of a *drama*; it is usually subdivided into *scenes.* In the 16th century English playwrights, due to the influence of Classical dramatists, divided their plays into five acts, but now playwrights tend to prefer the three-act form. Many modern playwrights have also written *one-act plays.*

acting time ['– – –]: the time from the beginning to the end of an *episode* presented in a *fictional* text. Usually acting time in an episode is longer than *narrating time*, because the writer can, in a few hundred words, describe the passing of years; cf. *mode of presentation.*

action ['ækʃn] (n.): in *fictional* texts, everything that happens in the story. Action may be on the level of physical reality (external action), when the writer describes what the *characters* do, or it may take place in the minds of the characters (internal action), when the writer shows the thoughts of the characters. Most *novels* combine both external and internal action to give an overall view of the characters and the *plot.*

adage ['ædɪdʒ] (n.): cf. *proverb.*

Aesthetic Movement [ɪs'θetɪk ☆ es-]: a movement which held that art should not be *didactic* and that beauty should be the sole ideal by which art is judged. "Art for art's sake" was the catchphrase of the movement. It was at its most influential in England during the 1880s, with Oscar Wilde its principal exponent.

alexandrine [ˌælɪg'zændraɪn ☆ -drɪn] (n.): in *poetry*, a *line* of *verse* consisting of six *iambic* feet (cf. *foot*), often with a pause (or *caesura*) after the third foot:
— ′— | — ′— | — ′— ‖ — ′— | — ′— | — ′—
In English poetry the alexandrine is normally called the iambic *hexameter*, and is rarely used.
Example: "Fierce wárs | and fáith|ful lóves ‖ shall mó|ralíze | my sóng"
(Edmund Spenser, THE FAIRIE QUEENE; 1590)

alienation effect [ˌeɪlɪə'neɪʃn ɪˌfekt] (n.): a principle in some modern *drama*, expounded by Bertolt Brecht, which states that both actors and audience should remain detached from a *play* and its performance. They should remember it is only a play and not identify with it. The sense of reality may be destroyed through such devices as addressing the audience directly, using a *chorus* to comment on the *action*, or interrupting the action.
Example: The use of a stage-manager to comment on the action in Thornton Wilder's play OUR TOWN (1938) destroys the sense of reality.

allegory ['ælɪgərɪ ☆ -gɔːriː] (n.), **allegorical** [ˌælɪ'gɒrɪkl ☆ -'gɔːr-] (adj.): a *fictional* text which may be understood on two levels – a superficial or factual level and a deeper, philosophical level – and in which the *characters* are usually personifications of abstract ideas or qualities and bear names which reveal the quality they represent, e.g. Trust, Vice. The term allegory may sometimes be extended to refer to any text in which characters or people represent abstract qualities. Through a simple storyline an allegory allows the reader to understand general concepts; cf. *fable, parable.*
Examples: John Bunyan's PILGRIM'S PROGRESS
(1678–1684), in which there are characters
such as Faithful and Giant Despair.
George Orwell's ANIMAL FARM (1945),
in which the animals represent
different types of thought and people.

alliteration [əˌlɪtə'reɪʃn] (n.), **alliterate** [ə'lɪtəreɪt] (v.): the *repetition* of a sound, normally a consonant, at the beginning of neighbouring words or of stressed syllables within such words to produce a *rhythmic* effect.

Round the rugged rock the ragged rascal ran.

6

Example: "Five *m*iles *m*eandering with a *m*azy *m*otion"
(Samuel Coleridge, "Kubla Khan"; 1816)

allusion [ə'luːʒn] (n.): a direct or indirect reference to some well-known historical person or event, saying, *proverb* or a line or sentence from a work of literature. An allusion is often used to reveal the writer's education.
Example: The title of Ernest Hemingway's *novel* FOR WHOM THE BELL TOLLS (1940) is an allusion to John Donne's "Meditation XVII" (1624). Here Donne's concept that "no man is an island" is transformed by Hemingway to imply that the loss of freedom in one place means the loss of freedom everywhere.

alternate rhyme [ɔːl'tɜːnət ☆ 'ɔːltər-] (n.): the *rhyme scheme* a b a b.
Example: "If I could write the beauty of your *eyes* (a)
and in fresh numbers number all your *graces* (b)
The age to come would say, 'This poet *lies*; (a)
Such heavenly touches n'er touched earthly *faces*.'" (b)
(William Shakespeare, "Sonnet 17"; 1593–1600)

ambiguity [ˌæmbɪ'ɡjuːətɪ] (n.), **ambiguous** [æm'bɪɡjʊəs] (adj.): the use of a word or expression to convey two or more distinct feelings; this occurs because words have not merely *denotations*, but also *connotations*.
Example: "These boughs shake against the cold"
(William Shakespeare, "Sonnet 73"; 1593–1600)
Here "shake against" suggests that the tree shivers because of the cold, but it also suggests that the tree makes a defiant gesture toward the cold.

amplification [ˌæmplɪfɪ'keɪʃn] (n.): the use of language as a means to extend, magnify or emphasize something, usually through some form of *repetition*.
Example: "Everything in Marseilles, and about Marseilles, had stared at the sky, and been stared at in return, until a staring habit had become universal there. Strangers were stared out of countenance by staring white houses, staring white walls, staring white streets, staring tracts of arid road, staring hills from which verdure was burnt away."
(Charles Dickens, LITTLE DORRIT; 1855–1857)

anacoluthon [ˌænəkəʊ'luːθɒn ☆ -ɑːn] (n.), pl. **anacolutha** [ˌænəkəʊ'luːθə]: an abrupt change in a sentence from one grammatical construction to another; the sentence begins in one way and ends in another. It is often used to display fear, worry or despair.
Example: The vase of roses reminded me, but why did he do it?

anacrusis [ˌænəˈkruːsɪs] (n.), pl. **anacruses** [ˌænəˈkruːsiːz]: in *poetry*, one or more syllables which do not form part of the regular *metre*.
Example: "Till dánger's tróubled níght depárt
And the stár of peáce retúrn."
(Thomas Campbell, "Ye Mariners of England"; ca. 1800)

anagnorisis [ˌænəgˈnɒrɪsɪs] (n.):
the recognition by a *character* in a literary work, especially a *tragedy*, of his or her true nature or of the truth about another character. This usually leads to the *denouement*. The term was coined by Aristotle in his work POETICS.

anapaest [ˈænəpest] (n.), **anapaestic** [ˌænəˈpestɪk] (adj.): a *metrical foot* consisting of two unstressed syllables followed by a stressed syllable: – – ' –
Examples: "I am món|arch of áll | I survéy "
(William Cowper, "Verses Supposed to be Written by Alexander Selkirk"; 1782)
"With a léap | and a bóund | the swift Án|apaests thróng."
(Samuel Coleridge, "Metrical Feet"; 1806)

anaphora [əˈnæfərə] (n.): the *repetition* of the same words in neighbouring sentences, *lines*, *stanzas*, etc., usually at the beginning of the clause. It is a form of *parallelism*, and is used to heighten the effect of the text. It is usually found in poems.
Example: "*In every* cry of every man,
In every infant's cry of fear,
In every voice, *in every* ban"
(William Blake, "London"; 1794)

anecdote [ˈænɪkdəʊt] (n.), **anecdotal** [ˌænɪkˈdəʊtl] (adj.): a simple, short and usually amusing or thought-provoking story about an incident relating to a person. An anecdote is usually passed on by word of mouth.
Example: When he was a boy, George Washington cut down his father's cherry tree. When asked by his father if he was the guilty one, the ever-truthful George Washington replied, "Father, I cannot tell a lie. I did it with my little hatchet."

Angry Young Men: a term used to describe a generation of post-war British writers who reacted against the bourgeois values of the establishment.

The best-known of these writers are Kingsley Amis (LUCKY JIM; 1954), John Braine (ROOM AT THE TOP; 1957), John Osborne (LOOK BACK IN ANGER; 1957) and John Wain (HURRY ON DOWN; 1953).

antagonist [æn'tægənɪst] (n.): in *fictional* texts, the person who opposes the *protagonist*.
Example: Macduff is Macbeth's antagonist in William Shakespeare's MACBETH (ca. 1606).

anticipation [æn,tɪsɪ'peɪʃn] (n.): cf. *foreshadowing*.

anti-climax [,æntɪ 'klaɪmæks] (n.): a sudden change from something noble or exciting to something banal or uninteresting. It usually occurs after *tension* has been building up in a text, and then the outcome does not match the reader's or listener's expectations. If used deliberately, it may have a humorous effect; cf. *bathos*.
Example: "Prince Bayard would have smashed his sword
To see the sort of knights you dub –
Is that the last of them – O Lord!
Will someone take me to a pub?"
(G.K. Chesterton, "A Ballade of an Anti-Puritan"; ca. 1900)

anti-hero ['æntɪ ,hɪərəʊ ☆ ,hɪr-] (n.): a *protagonist* who lacks the traditional heroic characteristics such as courage and bravery, does not carry out great deeds and does not fit into conventional society. The anti-hero became very popular in 20th-century literature; cf. *hero*.
Examples: Charles Lumley in John Wain's HURRY ON DOWN (1953)
Willy Loman in Arthur Miller's DEATH OF A SALESMAN (1949)

anti-novel ['æntɪ ,nɒvl ☆ ,nɑːvl] (n.): a kind of *fiction* that does not conform with traditional story-telling methods. This can be achieved through *digressions*, lack of *plot* and structural *order*, etc.
Example: James Joyce, ULYSSES (1922)

antiphrasis [æn'tɪfrəsɪs] (n.), pl. **antiphrases** [æn'tɪfrəsiːz]: the use of a word in a sense opposite to its normal meaning, especially for *ironic* effect.

antithesis[1] [æn'tɪθɪsɪs] (n.), **antithetic(al)** [,æntɪ'θetɪk(l)] (adj.): a stylistic device characterized by arranging opposing ideas in the form of grammatically similar or identical constructions, thus emphasizing the *contrast*; cf. *chiasmus*.
Examples: "The *faults* of women are visited as *sins*; the *sins* of men are not even visited as *faults*."
(Caroline Norton, THE WIFE AND WOMAN'S REWARD; 1835)

"There is no *king* who has not had a *slave* among his ancestors,
and no *slave* who has not had a *king* among his."
(Helen Keller, THE STORY OF MY LIFE; 1902)

antithesis[2] (n.): cf. *dialectical order.*

anti-utopia [ˌæntɪ juːˈtəʊpjə] (n.), **anti-utopian** [ˌ– – – ˈ– –] (adj.): in a *fictional*
text, a futuristic and perfectly organized world, in which individual freedom
is severely limited. Anti-utopian literature usually intends to warn the reader
about the dangers of any form of totalitarianism. Another term for anti-utopia
is "dystopia".
Examples: Ray Bradbury, FAHRENHEIT 451 (1953)
George Orwell, 1984 (1949)
Aldous Huxley, BRAVE NEW WORLD (1932)

aphorism [ˈæfərɪzm] (n.), **aphoristic** [ˌ– – ˈ– –] (adj.): a short, usually witty,
statement containing a truth or dogma.
Examples: "If a man will begin with certainties, he shall end in doubts; but if
he will be content to begin with doubts, he shall end in
certainties."
(Francis Bacon, THE ADVANCEMENT OF LEARNING; 1605)
"God helps them that help themselves."
(Benjamin Franklin, POOR RICHARD'S ALMANAC; 1736)

apocalyptic literature [əˌpɒkəˈlɪptɪk ☆ -ˌpɑːk-]: literature which deals with future
events of a destructive nature, especially concerning the end of the world.
The term is derived from the Book of the Apocalypse in the Bible, which
describes the end of the world and the Day of Judgment.
Examples: Nevil Shute, ON THE BEACH (1957)
Robert O'Brien, Z FOR ZACHARIAH (1975)

apology [əˈpɒlədʒɪ ☆ -ˈpɑːl-] (n.), **apologetic** [əˌpɒləˈdʒetɪk ☆ -ˌpɑːl-] (adj.): a work
written to defend or explain one's beliefs, ideas or opinions.
Examples: J.H. Newman's APOLOGIA PRO VITA SUA (1864) is a defence of
his Catholicism.
Sir Philip Sidney, APOLOGY FOR POETRY (1580)

apostrophe [əˈpɒstrəfɪ ☆ -ˈpɑːs-] (n.): a stylistic device whereby a writer or
character in a text addresses an absent or dead person, an abstract idea or
something non-human.
Examples: "BRUTUS: O Julius Caesar! thou art mighty yet:
Thy spirit walks abroad, and turns our swords
In our own proper entrails."
(William Shakespeare, JULIUS CAESAR, V, iii, 94–96; ca. 1599)

"LEAR: Blow, winds, and crack your cheeks! rage! blow!
You cataracts and hurricanoes, spout
Till you have drench'd our steeples, drown'd the cocks!"
(William Shakespeare, KING LEAR, III, ii, 1–3; ca. 1605)

archetype ['ɑːkɪtaɪp] (n.), **archetypal** [,– – '– –] (adj.): a *character* or event that is so typical and universal that the reader or audience identifies with him, her or it without requiring an explanation. A femme fatale, the wise old man, a quest or a father-son struggle may all be considered archetypal.

argumentation [,ɑːgjʊmen'teɪʃn] (n.), **argumentative** [,– – '– – –] (adj.): one of the five *text types*; an argumentative text deals with ideas and controversy, and expresses a clear opinion, providing reasons for it.

argumentum ad hominem (Lat. "appeal to the man"): an appeal by the *author* directly to the reader in which he or she arouses interest in and pity for his or her *characters*, by using *emotive language*.
Example: "If you think ... that anything like a romance is preparing for you, reader, you never were more mistaken ... Do you expect passion, and stimulus, and melodrama? Calm your expectations; reduce them to a lowly standard. Something real, cool, and solid lies before you; something unromantic as Monday morning."
(Charlotte Brontë, SHIRLEY; 1849)

aside [ə'saɪd] (n.): words spoken by a *character* in a *play* which the audience, but not the other characters, are supposed to hear. An aside reveals the thoughts and intentions of the character, and usually contrasts with the words which he or she speaks to the other characters. It can also be used to comment, usually in a humorous way, on the *action* of the play.
Example: "POLONIUS: [*Aside*] Though this be madness, yet there is method in 't. – Will you walk out of the air, my lord?
HAMLET: Into my grave?
POLONIUS: Indeed, that is out o' the air. – [*Aside*] How pregnant sometimes his replies are!"
(William Shakespeare, HAMLET, II, ii, 206–210; ca. 1601) Polonius's asides reveal his true reactions to Hamlet's apparent madness.

assonance ['æsənəns] (n.): the *repetition* of the same or similar vowel sounds within stressed syllables of neighbouring words.
Examples: "A miner on the d*o*le,
with n*o*where to g*o*"
(Bryn Griffiths, "On the Dole"; 1969)
"tw*i*ce f*i*ve m*i*les of fert*i*le ground"
(Samuel Coleridge, "Kubla Khan"; 1816)

atmosphere ['ætməs‚fɪə] (n.): a feeling or mood created by a writer in his or her work. It may be, for example, pleasant or gloomy, peaceful or violent; cf. *tone*.

attitudinal adverb [‚ætɪ'tjuːdɪnl ☆ -ə'tuːd-]: an adverb which expresses a writer's attitude towards his or her topic or subject, e.g. "honestly", "obviously"; cf. *intensifying adverb*.
Example: The Prime Minister is *obviously* concerned about ...

author ['ɔːθə] (n.): a person who writes either *fictional* or *non-fictional prose* texts. In fictional texts, the author is rarely to be identified with the *narrator*.

autobiography [‚ɔːtəʊbaɪ'ɒgrəfɪ ☆ -'ɑːg-] (n.), **autobiographical** [‚ɔːtəʊbaɪə'græfɪkl] (adj.): a person's own account of his or her life; sometimes it may be a mixture of *fiction* and *non-fiction*; cf. *biography*.
Example: Benjamin Franklin's AUTOBIOGRAPHY (1771) is a description of his rise from poverty to wealth, and he recommends it as a guide for others to follow.

avant-garde [‚ævɒŋ 'gɑːd ☆ ‚ɑːvɑːn] (n. and adj.): a term referring to literature based on the newest methods and ideas, and which is normally of an unorthodox and unconventional nature.

B

ballad ['bæləd] (n.): a *rhyming* story in the form of a song or *poem*. It normally has a strong dramatic element and a noble or *tragic tone*. There is usually a *refrain*, and the story is related by an *omniscient narrator*.
Example: Samuel Coleridge, "The Rime of the Ancient Mariner" (1798)

bathos ['beɪθɒs ☆ -ɑːs] (n.), **bathetic** [bə'θetɪk] (adj.): sudden change from the elevated or sublime to the ridiculous or foolish. Bathos is usually used to refer to examples that are unintentional, whereas *anti-climax* is used to refer to examples that are deliberate.
Example: "She lived unknown, and few could know
When Lucy ceased to be,
But she is in her grave, and, oh,
The difference to me."
(William Wordsworth, "Lucy"; ca. 1799)

Beat poets: a group of American poets in the 1950s and 1960s who rejected middle-class American values in favour of non-materialistic ideals. Many of them experimented with drugs and Eastern mysticism, or travelled across America in search of themselves – this resulted in the birth of the "road novel", as exemplified by Jack Kerouac's ON THE ROAD (1957). Other famous beat poets include Allen Ginsberg and William S. Burroughs.

biography [baɪ'ɒgrəfɪ ☆ -'ɑːg-] (n.), **biographical** [ˌ– – '– – –] (adj.): an account of a person's life history, written by another person; cf. *autobiography*.
Example: Mrs Gaskell, LIFE OF CHARLOTTE BRONTË (1857)

black comedy [ˌ– '– – –]: a type of *comedy* (or any other kind of literature) which displays humanity in such an absurd and hopeless situation that one is forced to laugh. Black comedy became widespread in the 20th century as part of a philosophical despair concerning human existence. "Black humour" is used to describe either the *style* in which black comedy is written or any particular *episode* in a text which is characterized by this form of absurdity.
Examples: Joseph Heller's CATCH 22 (1961), in which war, death and suffering are the objects of *humour*.
Samuel Beckett, WAITING FOR GODOT (1955)

black humour ☆ **humor** ['hjuːmə]: cf. *black comedy*.

blank verse [ˌ– '–]: unrhymed *verse* consisting of five *iambic* feet (cf. *foot*), also called the iambic *pentameter*; it was introduced into England in the 16th century and is widely used in English *poetry*, since it is close to the *rhythmic* patterns of English *speech*. However it is difficult to find blank verse which strictly follows the iambic *metre*.

Examples: "Which trémb|ling stúck,| and shóok | withín | the síde:
Wherewíth | the cáves | gan hól|lowly | resóund"
(Henry Howard, Earl of Surrey, VIRGIL'S AENEID, The Trojan Horse, II, 69–70; ca. 1557)
"This róy|al thróne | of kíngs,| this scép|ter'd ísle,
This eárth | of má|jesty,| this seát | of Márs"
(William Shakespeare, RICHARD II, II, i, 40–41; ca. 1595)
Notice how in both examples the second *line* does not strictly adhere to the iambic metre.

burlesque [bɜː'lesk] (n.): a literary work, especially a *drama*, which makes its subject ridiculous through *exaggeration*. Frequently a burlesque imitates and makes fun of a literary work, and it may also deal with and mock a particular set of people, ideas or beliefs.

C

cacophony [kəˈkɒfənɪ ☆ kæˈkɑːf-] (n.): the use of harsh or ugly sounds, usually in *poetry*, to produce a certain effect. Cacophony can be achieved especially through the use of words that contain plosive consonants (e.g. b, d, g, p, t, k)
    Example: "Hear the loud alarum bells
        Brazen bells! What a tale of terror now, their turbulency tells!"
        (Edgar Allan Poe, "The Bells"; 1849)

caesura [sɪˈzjʊərə ☆ -ˈzʊr-] (n.): a natural pause or break in a *line* of *verse*.
    Example: "To be or not to be: ‖ that is the question"
        (William Shakespeare, HAMLET, III, i, 56; ca. 1601)

canto [ˈkæntəʊ] (n.): the main division of a long *narrative poem*, similar to a chapter in a *novel*.

caricature [ˈkærɪkəˌtjʊə ☆ -ˌtʃʊr] (n.): in any *fictional* text, a *character* portrayal in which certain traits of the character have been exaggerated to produce a *comic* effect.
    Examples: Sir Toby Belch in William Shapespeare's TWELFTH NIGHT (ca. 1600), who is depicted as a vulgar drunk (hence his name)
        Lady Bracknell in Oscar Wilde's THE IMPORTANCE OF BEING EARNEST (1895), who is depicted as an extremely haughty and insensitive aristocrat.

carol [ˈkærəl ☆ ˈker-] (n.): a festive Christmas song. It originally meant a ring-dance accompanied by a song. In medieval literature there are carols for many different occasions.

carpe diem [ˌkɑːpɪ ˈdiːem] (Lat. "seize the day"): a *motif* recurring in literature, which invites the reader to enjoy life while he or she can. The term is taken from the Roman poet Horace's ODES.

cartoon [kɑːˈtuːn] (n.): a *comic* or *satirical* drawing, often dealing with current, especially political, events.

catachresis [ˌkætəˈkriːsɪs] (n.): the misapplication of a word, especially in a *mixed metaphor*. It can also be used to denote words used in an incorrect sense, e.g. "luxuriant" instead of "luxurious". An exaggerated form of catachresis is known as a *malaproprism*.

catastrophe [kə'tæstrəfɪ] (n.): the *tragic denouement* of a *play* or story, in which the outcome (usually the death of the *hero*) is presented.

catharsis [kə'θɑːsɪs] (n.): the release of certain of the audience's emotions while watching a *tragedy*. Aristotle, in his definition of tragedy in POETICS, wrote that "tragedy through pity or fear causes a catharsis (i.e. purgation) of such emotions." In other words, when watching a tragedy, the audience has its emotions, especially those of pity and fear, aroused; and then, through the c*limax* and *catastrophe*, these emotions are released. After the *tension* there follows a sense of calm.

character ['kærəktə] (n): in a *fictional* text, a person developed through action, *description*, language and way of speaking; cf. *flat character, round character.*

characterization [ˌ– – – – '– –] (n.), **characterize** ['– – – –] (v.): the way of presenting a *character* in a *fictional* text; cf. *explicit characterization, implicit characterization.*

chiasmus [kaɪ'æzməs] (n.), pl. **chiasmi** [-maɪ]: a *stylistic* device in which the main elements of the first half of a sentence are gramatically reversed in the second half of the sentence; cf. *antithesis[1]*.
Example: "Love's fire heats water, water cools not love."
      (William Shakespeare, "Sonnet 154"; 1593–1600)

chorus[1] ['kɔːrəs] (n.): an actor or actors who comment on a *play* during its performance or recite the *prologue* or *epilogue*, but who otherwise take no part in the *action*. Choruses were a fundamental part of Greek *drama*, but have rarely been used since. The chorus's commentary became incorporated

into the play through minor *characters*, the use of *soliloquies*, etc. In *Elizabethan* and modern drama, choruses are occasionally found; in the latter they are used either to add *atmosphere* or as part of the *alienation effect*.
Examples: The chorus of women in T. S. Eliot's MURDER IN THE CATHEDRAL
(1935)
The Stage-Manager in Thornton Wilder's OUR TOWN (1938)

chorus[2]: cf. *refrain*.

chronological order [ˌkrɒnəˈlɒdʒɪkl ☆ ˌkrɑːnəˈlɑː-]: a simple *temporal order*, in which the *action* of a literary work is presented in the sequence as it actually occurred or is supposed to have occurred.

Classicism [ˈklæsɪsɪzm] (n.): a style of literature in which the *themes* and conventions of ancient Greek and Roman (also called Classical) writers were used by European writers between the 16th and 18th centuries; cf. *Enlightenment, Neoclassicism*.

cliché [ˈkliːʃeɪ ☆ – ˈ–] (n.): a commonplace, over-used expression which retains little or none of its original meaning.
Examples: in the political wilderness
(to) add insult to injury

climactic order [klaɪˈmæktɪk]: the structuring of a text in such a way that the items or events dealt with become increasingly important and lead to a *climax*.

climax [ˈklaɪmæks] (n.), **climactic** [klaɪˈmæktɪk] (adj.): a structural element of a text, usually the moment when the *conflict* is most intense. In *fictional* texts, the climax follows the *rising action* and precedes the *turning point*; cf. *plot*.

comedy [ˈkɒmədɪ ☆ ˈkɑːm-] (n.): a kind of *drama* which deals with a light topic or a more serious one in an amusing way. A comedy always has a happy ending and usually makes fun of what is ridiculous and absurd. Comedy rarely deals with evil or wickedness – when it does it is usually as *black comedy*. Comedies rarely have noble *heroes* and heroines; rather the central *characters* are ordinary, down-to-earth people. Comedy may be divided into many categories, amongst which are (a) *romantic* comedy, which deals with lovers overcoming obstacles in order to be united, (b) *satirical* comedy, which aims to criticize society, (c) *farce* and (d) *comedy of manners*.

Examples: William Shakespeare, A MIDSUMMER NIGHT'S DREAM (ca. 1596)
William Shakespeare, AS YOU LIKE IT (ca. 1599)
Richard Sheridan, THE SCHOOL FOR SCANDAL (1777)

comedy of manners: a kind of *comedy*, the main subject and *theme* of which are the behaviour and way of life of certain social classes, in particular the middle and upper classes, which it portrays and lightly satirizes through witty *dialogue* and sophisticated *humour*.
Example: Oscar Wilde, THE IMPORTANCE OF BEING EARNEST (1895)

comic ['kɒmɪk ☆ 'kɑːm-] (adj.): inducing laughter or amusement. Whereas *comedy* usually refers to *drama*, comic can be used to describe other forms of literature, e.g. comic *novel*, comic *poem*.

comic relief [rɪ'liːf]: a *comic episode* or episodes in a serious *drama*, especially a *tragedy*, which aim to relieve the *tension* by amusing the audience, but which also reinforce the tragic elements through *contrast*. They also add to the *suspense* by delaying the development of the *action*.
Example: The Porter *scene[1]* (II, iii, 1–41) in William Shakespeare's MACBETH (ca. 1606)

coming-of-age story: a *fictional* text, in which the process of growing up is portrayed. Usually the *hero* or heroine is a child or adolescent, who in the course of the story undergoes an experience which changes his or her outlook on life and marks a important stage in his or her development. The coming-of-age story is sometimes referred to as the "story of initiation".
Examples: Doris Lessing, "Through the Tunnel" (1954)
Sherwood Anderson, "I Want to Know Why" (ca. 1920)

comment ['kɒmənt ☆ 'kɑːm-] (n.): a *non-fictional text form* belonging to the *text type argumentation,* in which the writer or speaker gives his or her personal opinion about a topic.

Commonwealth period ['kɒmənwelθ ☆ 'kɑːm-]: a period in British history, lasting from 1649 to 1660, when there was no monarch. The country was ruled by a Puritan Parliament under Oliver Cromwell. During this time all public theatres were closed on moral grounds, and so little *drama* was written. Associated with this period are John Milton's political works and Thomas Hobbes's LEVIATHAN (1651).

conceit [kən'siːt] (n.): a stylistic device often including *metaphor, simile* and *hyperbole* to appeal to the reader's intellect by forming a connection between two seemingly dissimilar things, thereby surprising and giving a new insight to the reader; cf. *Metaphysical poets.*

Example: John Donne's *poem* "The Flea" (1633; in which the *speaker* urges his lover to accept him on the grounds that a flea has sucked blood from both of them)

concrete poem ['kɒŋkriːt]: a type of *poem* in which the words form a shape or a picture. Also known as "pattern poems", they have become quite popular in the 20th century.
Example: Reinhard Döhl, "Apple" (1967)

conflict ['kɒnflɪkt ☆ 'kɑːn-] (n.): a struggle or opposition between different forces which produces *tension*; cf. *external conflict, internal conflict.*

connotation [ˌkɒnə'teɪʃn ☆ ˌkɑːn-] (n.): additional meaning of a word beyond its dictionary definition; connotations arise due to the associations a word can form through personal or general human experience; cf. *denotation.*
Example: A "forest" is a place where many trees grow, but in the human mind it may connote "fear", "mystery", "confusion" or even "tranquillity", etc.

consonance ['kɒnsənəns ☆ 'kɑːns-] (n.): the *repetition* of the same consonant sounds before and after differing vowels; cf. *imperfect rhyme.*
Examples: knick-knack; ship-shape; creak/croak;
"Having seen all things *red*,
Their eyes are *rid*"
(Wilfred Owen, "Insensitivity"; 1918)

contrast ['kɒntrɑːst ☆ 'kɑːntræst] (n.): the bringing together of opposing views or words in order to emphasize their difference and heighten the feeling.
Example: "Roses have thorns, and silver fountains mud;
Clouds and eclipses stain both moon and sun,
And loathsome canker lives in sweetest bud.
All men make faults, ..."
(William Shakespeare, "Sonnet 35"; 1593–1600)
Contrast is used here to show that no one is perfect.

contrastive order [– ˌ– – ˈ– –] (n.): the structuring of a text to reflect opposing views by contrasting them throughout the text.

Example:	"Evil	Good
	I am cast upon a horrible desolate island, void of all hope of recovery.	But I am alive, and not drowned as all my ship's company was.
	I have not clothes to cover me.	But I am in a hot climate, where if I had clothes I could hardly wear them."

(Daniel Defoe, ROBINSON CRUSOE; 1719)

counterpoint ['kaʊntə,pɔɪnt] (n.): the use of more than one type of *foot* in a *line* of *poetry*. This is very common in English poetry.
Example: "Néver did sún more béautifully stéep
In his fírst spléndour válley, róck or híll,
Né'er sáw I, néver félt, a cálm so déep"
(William Wordsworth, "Composed upon Westminster Bridge"; 1802)
Here the basic foot is *iambic*, but other types of foot are included.

couplet ['kʌplət] (n.): two successive rhyming *lines*; couplets may be used throughout a *poem* or to end a *sonnet* or *monologue*; cf. *heroic couplet*.
Example: "But if the while I think on thee, dear *friend*
All losses are restor'd, and sorrows *end*."
(William Shakespeare, "Sonnet 30"; 1593–1600)

crisis ['kraɪsɪs] (n.), pl. **crises** ['kraɪsiːz]: the point in a text at which the *tension* reaches its maximum; from this point onwards it is clear what direction the *action* is going to take, because the *protagonist* usually makes an important decision during the crisis. The terms crisis and *turning point* are interchangeable in *tragedy*.

cynicism ['sɪnɪsɪzm] (n.), **cynical** ['– – –] (adj.): an attitude which is contemptuous of humanity, life and the world in general. It is based on an essentially sceptical attitude towards human values and is usually found in *satire* and *black humour*.
Example: "the kindest thing one can do to a native is to let him die"
(E.M. Forster, A PASSAGE TO INDIA; 1922–1924)

WHAT'S SO CYNICAL ABOUT HELPING THE POOR MAN SOLVE HIS PROBLEMS!

NO HOME NO JOB SPARE A PENNY

D

dactyl ['dæktɪl] (n.), **dactylic** [– '– –] (adj.): a *metrical foot* consisting of one stressed syllable followed by two unstressed syllables: '– – – . Because it is unlike natural English *rhythmic* patterns, it is rare to find a *poem* composed entirely of dactyls.
Example: "Cánnon to | ríght of them
Cánnon to | léft of them
Cánnon in | frónt of them"
(Lord Tennyson, "The Charge of the Light Brigade"; 1855)

dead metaphor ['metəfə]: a *metaphor* that has been used so often that it has lost its *symbolic* meaning; cf. *cliché.*
Examples: gilded youth
the heart of the matter

delineation [dɪ‚lɪnɪ'eɪʃn] (n.), **delineate** [dɪ'lɪnɪeɪt] (v.): a *description* of somebody or something in sharp detail.

denotation [‚– – '– –] (n.): the actual definition of a word; cf. *connotation.*
Example: "forest" means "an area of land covered with growing trees"

denouement [‚deɪ'nuːmõ ☆ ‚deɪnuː'mãː] (n.): the final outcome of a *fictional* text, especially in a *drama*, when the *conflict* is resolved. In *tragedy*, the denouement may be the *hero's* or heroine's destruction or his or her failure to achieve his or her goals; in *comedy*, it may be the restoration of the hero's or heroine's fortunes or the accomplishment of his or her goals. Denouement is also known as "solution"; cf. *plot* and *open ending*; cf. *catastrophe.*

description [– '– –] (n.), **descriptive** [– '– –] (adj.): one of the five *text types*; a descriptive text presents the physical characteristics of living things, objects and/or processes; cf. *impressionistic description, technical description.*

deus ex machina [‚deɪʊs eks 'mækɪnə ☆ 'maːkɪnaː] (n.) (Lat., "god out of a machine"): an unexpected event or intervention in a *play* or *novel* which resolves a problem or a difficulty. It is often used to contrive a "happy ending". In England, it occurs mostly in pre-20th-century literature. The name derives from the device in Greek *drama* whereby a god was lowered onto the stage by a sort of machine in order to untangle a difficult *plot.*
Examples: In Charles Dickens's OLIVER TWIST (1837–1838) the boy Oliver turns out to be the nephew of the lady who cares for him.
Oscar Wilde parodies the device in THE IMPORTANCE OF BEING

EARNEST (1895), when John Worthing discovers he can marry Gwendolen, because his long-lost nanny reveals that his baptismal name is Ernest.

dialectical order [ˌdaɪəˈlektɪkl]: the structuring of a text by opening with the statement of an idea or *action* (thesis), following it with its opposite (antithesis) and solving the *conflict* between the two in a compromise (synthesis). It is most often used in *argumentative* texts.

dialogue [ˈdaɪəlɒg ☆ -lɔːg] (n.): two or more people speaking to each other in any kind of text.

diary [ˈdaɪərɪ] (n.): a personal record of facts and/or experiences written at frequent intervals (usually daily). A diary is normally factual, but ocassionally writers use the diary form to present a *fictional* story; cf. *journal*.
Examples: (factual) Pepys, DIARY (ca. 1660)
(story told in diary form) Robert O'Brien, Z FOR ZACHARIAH (1975)

diatribe [ˈdaɪətraɪb] (n.): a violent verbal or written attack on a person or work.

didactic [daɪˈdæktɪk] (adj.): intended to teach or instruct. A didactic work encourages the reader or audience to lead a good life or to believe in or follow a particular philosophy, religion, etc. Some *text forms* are specifically intended to be didactic, e.g. *parables*; cf. *instruction*.

digression [daɪˈgreʃn] (n.): material in a literary work which is not strictly relevant to the main *plot* or *theme* of that work. Digressions are often used to relieve *tension* in a work or to provide humorous *episodes* to entertain the reader.

22

direct characterization [– ‚– ‚– – – – ' – –]: cf. *explicit characterization.*

document ['dɒkjʊmənt ☆ 'dɑːkjə-] (n.): any piece of writing that provides information about or evidence of an event.

drama ['drɑːmə] (n.): any work meant to be performed on a stage or as a film. Unlike most other forms of literature, a drama involves a visual element and relies upon the spoken words of the individual *characters*. Because drama is visual it relies on the *suspension of disbelief* on the part of the audience; that is, the audience (in most but not all cases; cf. *alienation effect*) must accept that they are watching real events. As drama involves spoken word and *action*, inner thoughts are usually revealed through *dialogue* and, in dramas of past centuries, *soliloquies*. The word drama today sometimes refers to a serious *play* as compared to a *comedy*. Drama was originally one of the three Greek *genres*, and is still a generic term, covering all forms of literature which are intended for visual production.

dramatic irony [– ‚– – ' – – –]: a device by which a *character's* words have a different meaning for the audience than for the character, because the audience knows some information which the character does not. In some cases, the words spoken by a character recoil on him or her later; cf. *tragic irony.*
    Example: In William Shakespeare's TWELFTH NIGHT (ca. 1600) Malvolio believes that Olivia has sent him a love letter and therefore he behaves in an excited and ridiculous manner; the audience, however, knows that the letter is a fake.

dramatis personae [‚dræmətɪs pɜːˈsəʊnaɪ ☆ -iː] (Lat. "*characters* of the *play*"): the characters in a *drama*; usually the list of names and status of the characters printed at the beginning of the play's text.

dramatized narrator ['dræmətaɪzd]: a *character* who tells the story in a *fictional* work or through whose eyes the events are witnessed. The dramatized narrator may be involved in the *action* or be a passive onlooker, and may tell the story in an unobtrusive manner or seek to analyse the events and other characters.

duologue ['djʊəlɒg ☆ 'duːələːg] (n.): a conversation between two *characters* in a work of literature; *dialogue* is usually used to cover the term duologue.

dystopia [dɪsˈtəʊpjə] (n.): cf. *anti-utopia.*

E

editorial [ˌedɪ'tɔːrɪəl] (n.): a variant of the *text form comment*. An editorial is usually written by the chief editor of a newspaper or magazine and contains a particular opinion on some topic of current importance or general concern. The views expressed are generally representative of the political leanings of the publication as a whole, and are written in language appropriate to the social background of the general reader. An editorial is also known in British English as a "leader" or "leading article".

Edwardian [ed'wɔːdjən] (adj.): referring to the reign of King Edward VII (1901–1910). It was an age of prosperity and of exuberance. Amongst the writers associated with this period are H.G. Wells, G.B. Shaw, E.M. Forster and Saki.

elegy ['elɪdʒɪ] (n.): a meditative *poem* with a sad *tone*, usually mourning the death of an individual.
Example: Thomas Gray, "Elegy Written in a Country Churchyard" (1751)

Elizabethan [ɪˌlɪzə'biːθn] (adj.): referring to the reign of Queen Elizabeth I (1558–1603). Many of England's greatest writers are associated with this age, e.g. William Shakespeare, Christopher Marlowe, Edmund Spenser.

ellipsis [ɪ'lɪpsɪs] (n.), pl. **ellipses** [ɪ'lɪpsiːz]: the shortening of sentences by dropping a word or words which can be understood from the context. Ellipsis is often used by poets to make their *poems* more compact and direct; the *images* and mood created are considered to be more important than the correct grammar.
Example: "Coming?" instead of "are you coming?"

emotive language [ɪ'məʊtɪv]: the use of words and expressions which have particular *connotations* in order to appeal to the reader's or listener's emotions and so influence him or her to react in a particular way.

empathy ['empəθɪ] (n.): the identification with an animate or inanimate object. The writer evokes from the reader participation with an object that he or she describes; this may be achieved through the use of words to produce a similar feeling to what is described.

Example: "High there, how he rung upon the rein of a wimpling wing
In his extasy! then off, off forth on swing"
(Gerald Manley Hopkins, "The Windhover"; 1877)
Here the reader senses the experience of the bird flying, first gliding and then soaring away.

empiricism [ɪm'pɪrɪsɪzm] (n.): the belief that experience and observation are the only sources of knowledge. Empiricism was an important concept in the *Enlightenment* because of its emphasis on the faculty of reason.

enclosed rhyme: the *rhyme scheme* a b b a.

end rhyme (n.): a *rhyme* which comes at the end of two *lines* of *verse*. The lines need not follow one after the other. This is the most conventional rhyme in *poetry*.

Example: "Two roads diverged in a yellow *wood*,
And sorry I could not travel both
And be one traveler, long I *stood*
And looked down as far as I *could*."
(Robert Frost, "The Road Not Taken"; 1916)

end-stopped line [ˌ– – '–]: a *line* of a *poem* or *verse*, at the end of which there is a pause, because a sentence or phrase has come to an end. Usually semi-colons or full-stops indicate an end-stopped line; cf. *enjambement*.

Example: "Ne'er saw I, never felt, a calm so so *deep*!
The river glideth at his own sweet *will*:
Dear God! the very houses seem *asleep*;
And all that mighty heart is lying *still*!"
(William Wordsworth, "Composed upon Westminster Bridge"; 1802)

enjambement [ɪn'dʒæmmənt] (n.): a sentence or a clause in a *poem* which runs on from one *line* to the next without a pause. It is also called a "run-on line".

Example: "Here at your sea-washed, sunset gates shall *stand*
A mighty woman with a torch, whose *flame*
Is the imprisoned lightning."
(Emma Lazarus, "The New Colossus"; 1883)

Enlightenment [ɪn'laɪtənmənt] (n.): a term used to describe an intellectual and cultural movement which developed in 17th- and 18th-century Europe. At the basis of Enlightenment philosophy was the belief in the powers of human reason. Authority and superstition were considered inadequate grounds on which to build philosophical and religious beliefs. Amongst the influential writers of this period were John Locke, Benjamin Franklin, Immanuel Kant and Voltaire; cf. *Classicism, Neoclassicism*.

entrance ['entrəns] (n.): in a *drama*, the coming of an actor or actress onto the stage.

envoy ['envɔɪ ☆ 'ɑːn-] (n.): a final *stanza* in a *poem* which is usually shorter than the preceding stanzas and often repeats the *refrain* of the poem. It is only used in certain types of poem and is rarely found in English *poetry*.

epic ['epɪk] (n. and adj.): a long, *narrative poem* about some historic or *mythical* event, usually the deeds and death of a *hero*. The epic belongs to ancient Classical *poetry*, but there are examples in English literature. It is normally elevated in *style* and serious in subject matter. Epic was one of the three Greek *genres*, and referred to *narrative* poetry; cf. *mock epic*.
Examples: John Milton, PARADISE LOST (1658–1663)
Alfred, Lord Tennyson, MORTE D'ARTHUR (1833–1834)

epigram ['epɪgræm] (n.), **epigrammatic(al)** [ˌepɪgrə'mætɪk(l)] (adj.): a short, witty statement, sometimes in *prose*, sometimes in *verse*.
Example: "To err is human, to forgive divine."
(Alexander Pope, "An Essay on Criticism"; 1711)

epigraph ['epɪgrɑːf ☆ -græf] (n.): a motto or quotation at the beginning of a text, especially of a *novel* or a chapter of a novel, revealing something important or interesting for the reader to consider when reading the text.

epilogue ['epɪlɒg ☆ -lɔːg] (n.): the concluding section of a literary work, in which it is revealed what happened to the *characters* after the *denouement*. An epilogue is also used to refer to a short *speech* delivered at the end of a *play*, and to the *moral* at the end of a *fable*.

episode ['epɪsəʊd] (n.): a (short) event, incident or *digression* within a longer *narrative* text.

epitaph ['epɪtɑːf ☆ -tæf] (n.): an inscription on a tomb or grave, usually giving a *description* of the person who lies buried there. An epitaph may also be a short *poem* or statement written about somebody who died some time before. It may be serious or flippant.
Example: "Here lies my wife: here let her rest
Now she's at rest and so am I."
(John Dryden on his wife)

epithet ['epɪθet] (n.): an adjective or short phrase characterizing the special quality of a person or thing.
Examples: Richard *the Lionheart*
  the *dark* continent (i.e. Africa)

essay ['eseɪ] (n.): a *text form* in which the writer expresses his or her personal views on some topic. Most essays can be said to represent either the *argumentative* or the *expository text types*; essays can vary widely in subject matter and *tone*, some being serious and others light-hearted and entertaining. They can also vary greatly in length. Although essays are usually works of *prose*, there are examples in *verse*.
Example: George Orwell, "Shooting an Elephant" (1950)

estrangement [ɪ'streɪndʒmənt] (n.): the result of the *alienation effect*, when the audience successfully distances itself emotionally from a *play* and is able to consider it more objectively and learn from it.

eulogy ['juːlədʒɪ] (n.): a statement or *speech* praising a person. It is also known as a "panegyric".
Example: "ANTHONY: This was the noblest Roman of them all ...
  His life was gentle, and the elements
  So mixed in him that Nature might stand up
  And say to all the world 'This was a Man!'"
  (Anthony's eulogy of Brutus in William Shakespeare's JULIUS CAESAR, V, v, 68, 73–75; ca. 1599)

euphemism ['juːfəmɪzm] (n.), **euphemistic** [ˌ‒ ‒ '‒ ‒] (adj.): a stylistic device used to hide the true nature of something unpleasant by expressing it in a more pleasant, less direct way.
Examples: "Needy", "underprivileged", "disadvantaged", "of a low socio-economic status" are all euphemisms for "poor".
  "To be helping the police with their inquiries" is a euphemism for "to be under close arrest on suspicion of having committed a crime".

euphony ['juːfənɪ] (n.): in any work of literature, the use of pleasant sounds. *Assonance* and long vowels are often part of euphony.
Example: "I caught this morning morning's minion, king-dom of
  daylight's dauphin, dapple-dawn-drawn Falcon, in his riding"
  (Gerald Manley Hopkins, "The Windhover"; 1877)

euphuism ['juːfjuːɪzm] (n.): an elaborate and affected use of language. It normally involves complicated sentence construction, *rhetorical questions*, *alliteration* and *assonance*. It is primarily associated with writers of the 16th and 17th centuries who attempted to exploit the *rhetorical* potential of the

English language through imitation of Classical writers, but the term may be applied to any text written in a highly elaborate *style*.

exaggeration [ɪɡ,zædʒə'reɪʃn] (n.): a strong overstatement; it may be used to draw the reader's attention to something horrible or in order to amuse the reader; cf. *hyperbole*.

Existentialism [ˌegzɪ'stenʃəlɪzm]: a philosophy made popular by the French writer Jean-Paul Sartre, which holds that people are born into a meaningless world and are free either to remain passive spectators on life or to transcend, or rise above, their situation through awareness of their meaningless existence. The choice between these two positions gives meaning to human existence. Actions determine people's natures rather than vice versa. Existentialism was very influential in the mid-20th century.

exit ['eksɪt] (n.): in a *drama*, the departure of a *character* from the stage. The plural of the verb "exit" is "exeunt" and is used only in the *stage directions*.

explicit characterization [ɪk'splɪsɪt]: a way of presenting a *character* directly. The *author* may provide a *description* of a character through the words of the *narrator* (especially an *omniscient narrator*), or another character in the text may comment on the character, or the character may describe himself or herself. Usually only an omniscient narrator's explicit characterization is objective and conclusive, since the other characters or the character him or herself may present the reader or audience with selected information, revealing only what they want to have known. Another term for explicit characterization is "direct characterization"; cf. *implicit characterization*.
Example: In F. Scott Fitzgerald's THE GREAT GATSBY (1925) the narrator gives a self-evaluation in the opening lines.

exposition[1] [ˌ– – '– –] (n.): a structural element of a *fictional* text, usually at the very beginning, which includes at least some of the following: the introduction of the main *character(s)*, the *theme*, the *setting*, the *atmosphere* or the *tone*. The exposition's purpose is to lead the reader/audience gently into the story. Often there is no exposition, so the reader/audience learns of the status of the characters, the setting, etc. through incidental details. Sometimes the exposition takes place after an *episode* or some *action*.
Example: "It is a truth universally acknowledged that a single man in possession of a good fortune must be in want of a wife."
(Jane Austen, PRIDE AND PREJUDICE; 1813)
The first sentence of this exposition reveals the theme (marriage) and the tone (*ironic*) of the *novel*.

28

exposition[2] (n.), **expository** [– '– – – –] (adj.): one of the five *text types*, in which the writer or speaker analyses and explains some relatively complex matter in an objective and precise way.

Expressionism [ɪk'spreʃənɪzm] (n.): a movement in art during the 19th and early 20th centuries which sought to portray a highly personal and psychological vision of the world as opposed to the depiction of external realities. Although it was mostly confined to German art, Expressionism did influence the works of several writers, e.g. Eugene O'Neill and T.S. Eliot.

external conflict [ek'stɜːnl]: in a *fictional* text, the clash between two or more *characters*, or one character and fate, nature or society; cf. *internal conflict*.

extrapolation [ek,stræpə'leɪʃn] (n.): the technique of working out and describing how the future will be on the basis of already known facts and on observations. Extrapolation is often the foundation for *utopian* and *anti-utopian* literature: the writer predicts and depicts a futuristic society through the exaggeration of certain aspects of his or her own, and thereby can criticize his or her own society by demonstrating what may happen in the future if contemporary society continues on a certain path.
Example: Ray Bradbury's FAHRENHEIT 451 (1953) is based on the dangers that could arise from the relentless pursuit of happiness.

eye-rhyme ['aɪ raɪm] (n.): a false *rhyme*, consisting of words which give the eye the impression of forming an exact rhyme because their spellings are similar, but which in fact do not possess identical sounds.
Examples: "Strong gongs groaning as the guns boom *far*,
Don John is going to *war*."
(G. K. Chesterton, "Lepanto"; 1915)
"Dull would he be of soul who could pass *by*
A sight so touching in its majes*ty*."
(William Wordsworth, "Composed Upon Westminster Bridge"; 1802)

F

fable ['feɪbl] (n.):
a *fictional
narrative* text,
normally short
in length, in
which animals
represent human
types or act like
human beings;
as such it is a
form of *allegory*.
Fables are usually

WHY DO WE ALWAYS HAVE TO PLAY THE BAD GUYS IN FABLES?

didactic, since they intend to teach a moral lesson, make a *satirical* comment, or illustrate some general truth. A *moral* may be understood from the text or, in the more traditional version of a fable, there is a moral tag (*epilogue*) at the end.

Examples: James Thurber's "The Shrike and the Chipmunks" (1945)
George Orwell's ANIMAL FARM (1945) may also be considered a type of fable.

faction ['fækʃn] (n.), **factional** ['– – –] (adj.): a term coined in the late 1960s to describe a form of *fiction* in which the writer takes a true-life story and mingles it with fiction to produce a highly personal and sometimes controversial account of the original story, since the writer gives the people motives and personalities they may not have had. The word is a mixture of the words "fact" and "fiction".

Examples: Truman Capote's IN COLD BLOOD (1966) is a factional account of a murder.
E. L. Doctorow's RAGTIME (1975), in which real-life people mingle with fictional *characters*.

fairy tale ['feəri teɪl ☆ 'feriː] (n.): a *narrative prose* text about the adventures, fortunes and misfortunes of a *hero* or heroine. They are often young *archetypal characters*, good-looking, strong and rich men or beautiful and warm-hearted women. Fairy tales usually begin "once upon a time" and end "and they all lived happily ever after". Besides the human characters, there are usually *mythical* beings such as fairies, gnomes, etc. The tales are to a degree moral, since good usually triumphs over evil.

Examples: "Little Red Riding Hood"; "Sleeping Beauty"

falling action [ˌ– – ˈ– –]: a structural element of a *fictional* text, marked by a reduction in the *suspense*. Normally it follows the *turning point* or *climax*. In a *tragedy*, the *protagonist's* fortunes are in decline, while in a *comedy* they are improving. The falling action precedes the *denouement*; cf. *plot*.

farce [fɑːs] (n.): a *play* intended to provoke roars of laughter through exaggerated physical actions, absurd situations, *slapstick* and improbable surprises in the form of unexpected appearances and disclosures. The *plot* is usually complicated, because in order to maintain the comical mood the *action* moves quickly. Sexual jokes and mistaken identities are often the *themes* of farce.

feature story [ˈfiːtʃə]: a variant of the *text form report*, written to arouse human interest in a particular story. A feature story concentrates on an individual case, but is intended to represent many similar cases; for example, in a report on unemployment, the feature story would concentrate on the life of one unemployed person, implying that life is similar for other unemployed people. The feature story is a popular form of journalism, since it is not as dry as straight news.

feminine rhyme [ˈfemɪnɪn]: a *rhyme* of two or three syllables in which the first syllable is stressed; cf. *masculine rhyme*.
Examples: bríghtly/líghtly; móther/bróther; séventeen/Lévantine

fiction [ˈfɪkʃn] (n.), **fictional** [ˈfɪkʃənl] (adj.): an imaginative work, in which the writer creates his or her own world or presents an invented *narrative*. The reader is expected to accept this world or story as existing or true, even though it may be different from the reader's own experience (cf. *suspension of disbelief*). Within a text there may be a mingling of fact and fiction; cf. *faction*.

fictitious [fɪkˈtɪʃəs] (adj.): invented or imagined by a writer, and not necessarily corresponding to the real world. Fictitious differs from the term *fictional* in that it means something is deliberately not true, whereas fictional means something belongs to the realms of the imagination; however, the two words are often used interchangeably.

figurative [ˈfɪɡərətɪv ☆ -jər-] (adj.): language used to *connote* something else. The meaning of a word is extended beyond its usual dictionary definition to indicate something else. *Images*, *metaphors*, *similes* and *symbols* are all examples of figurative language, cf. *literal*.
Example: "(To) grit one's teeth" literally means "(to) press one's teeth together" (usually when one is in pain) but it is used figuratively to mean "(to) show determination in a difficult situation".

first person narrator: a *narrator* who is a *character* in a story. In the text the *author* uses "I" to identify the narrator. This narrator may be either the *protagonist* or a minor character (who acts as a sort of witness to the *action*). First person *narration* is a limited form of narration, since it presents the action through the eyes of one character only, so the information presented to the reader is selected. Despite the use of "I", the first person narrator is not to be confused with the author.

Example: "If you really want to hear about it, the first thing you'll probably want to know is where *I* was born, and what *my* lousy childhood was like, and how *my* parents were occupied and all before they had *me*, and all that David Copperfield kind of crap, but *I* don't feel like going into it."
(J.D. Salinger, THE CATCHER IN THE RYE; 1951)

five w's [faɪv ˈdʌbljuːz]: the five question words "who?", "what?", "when?", "where?" and "why?", which should provide factual, verifiable answers. They are an important part of journalistic *reports*, since they form the basis on which to write a report.

flashback [ˈflæʃbæk] (n.): an *episode* which interrupts the *chronological order* of a text in order to go back in time and show what happened earlier. Flashbacks are used to reveal new information, which had previously been hidden from the reader, at selected places so that the reader may understand a *character's* motivation better.

Example: Arthur Miller's DEATH OF A SALESMAN (1949), in which Willy Loman looks back upon his life.

flat character [‚– ˈ– – –]: a term coined by E.M. Forster in ASPECTS OF THE NOVEL (1927) to denote a minor *character* in a literary work who does not develop in the course of the *action*. A flat character is normally constructed around a single idea or quality; cf. *round character, stock character*.

foil [fɔɪl] (n.): a *character* in a piece of writing who serves as a contrast to another character (usually the *protagonist*), thus emphasizing the other character's traits.

Examples: Banquo is Macbeth's foil in William Shakespeare's MACBETH (ca. 1606).
Laertes is Hamlet's foil in William Shakespeare's HAMLET (ca. 1601).

foot [fʊt] (n.), pl. **feet** [fiːt]: a group of stressed and unstressed syllables within a *line* of *poetry* which forms a *metrical* unit.

The most common feet used in English poetry are:
a) *iamb*:   – ˈ–   e.g. avóid
b) *trochee*:   ˈ– –   e.g. háppen

c) *dactyl*:   '– – –   e.g. mérrily
d) *anapaest*:   – – '–   e.g. underneáth
e) *spondee*:   '– '–   e.g. hélp! hélp!
Samuel Coleridge's *poem*, "Metrical Feet" (1806), contains examples of the various feet:
"Tróchee | tríps from | lóng to |shórt.
From lóng | to lóng | in sól|emn sórt
Slów spón|dée stálks;| stróng fóot | yét ill | áble
Éver to | cóme up with the | dáctyl tri|sýllable
Iám|bics márch | from shórt | to lóng.
With a léap | and a bóund | the swift án|apaests thróng."
Note that the lines do not always contain the precise feet which they are describing.

foreshadowing [fɔːˈʃædəʊɪŋ] (n.): the technique of hinting at later events in a *fictional* text in such a way that the reader or spectator is prepared for them or can even anticipate them. In the *exposition* of a *novel* there is usually some idea of the *theme* and outcome of the story. This gives structural unity to a text, as well as lending it a certain degree of *tension*. Foreshadowing is also known as "anticipation".
    Examples: In Jane Austen's PRIDE AND PREJUDICE (1813) we suspect, from the first chapter's contents, that Elizabeth will suceed in marrying Mr. Bingley.
            In William Shakespeare's MACBETH (ca. 1606) the three witches allow the audience to believe that Macbeth will become king.

form [fɔːm] (n.): the way in which a literary work is shaped and structured. Form includes sentence structure and choice of words. Form and *substance* are the two ingredients in every text.

formal style [ˈfɔːml]: a use of language addressed to the educated reader or listener. Formal style shows detachment and respect for the intellect of the reader or listener and makes use of precise and often difficult vocabulary and verb forms and complex sentence construction. It is used most often in the *text form report*; cf. *informal style, style.*

frame story [ˈfreɪm ˌstɔːrɪ]: a story which contains one or more quite independent stories within it. The main story provides the frame for the other stories.
    Example: Geoffrey Chaucer's CANTERBURY TALES (ca. 1387), in which the main story is the journey of the pilgrims. During their journey, each of the pilgrims tells a story in turn.

free verse [ˌfriː ˈvɜːs]: a kind of *poem* whose structure is not established by a particular *rhyme scheme* or a regular *metre*, but by some other means, such as *repetition, anaphora, alliteration* or *assonance* or the selected mixing of stressed and unstressed syllables. It is largely a 20th-century phenomenon. Examples: "First, feel, then feel, then
read, or read, then feel, then
fall, or stand, where you
already are ..."
(Imamu Amiri Baraka, "Young Soul"; 1969)
"He stood by the bar,
squat, flat-capped, still strong
at fifty but condemned to
the scrapheap of industry's waste."
(Bryn Griffiths, "On the Dole"; 1969)

G

genre ['ʒɑːnrə] (n.): a literary classification. The three Classical genres are: *lyric* or poetic (spoken in the first person), *epic* or *narrative* (spoken by the *narrator* in the first person, but by the *characters* in their own voices), *dramatic* (spoken by the characters). These categories were later added to and subdivided, so that *novel*, *essay* and *short story* are also referred to as genres of literature.

Gothic ['gɒθɪk ☆ 'gɑːθ-] (adj.): a term used to describe a type of romance popular in Britain in the 18th and 19th centuries. The Gothic *novel* or story usually has a medieval *setting* and an *atmosphere* of mystery and horror.
Examples: Mary Shelley, FRANKENSTEIN (1818)
Edgar Allan Poe, "The Masque of the Red Death" (1842)

gradation [grə'deɪʃn]: a stylistic device in which a number of propositions are set forth in a series so that each one rises above the preceding in force leading to a climax. *Repetition* is normally a characteristic of gradation.
Example: "We shall *learn* all these devices the white man has,
We shall *handle* his tools for ourselves.
We shall *master* his machinery, his inventions, ..."
(Dave Martin Nez, "New Way, Old Way"; 1969)

grotesque [grəʊ'tesk] (adj., n.): any aberration or distortion in a *fictional* text; the ridiculous, macabre, bizarre, and unnatural may all be considered elements that belong to the grotesque. *Caricatures* are often grotesque, as are *episodes* that contain *black humour*. The grotesque is often used to shock, amuse or satirize.
Example: In Charles Dickens's NICHOLAS NICKLEBY (1838–1839) the cruel schoolmaster Wackford Squeers is depicted in a grotesque fashion.

H

hamartia [hɑ:'mɑ:ʃə] (n.): an error of judgment by a *character*, usually the *protagonist*, in a *drama*. The error is caused by a certain flaw or weakness in the character rather than by moral wickedness. Hamartia is often called the "tragic flaw". The character will break a moral law or commit a fatal error that leads to his or her downfall. The term was coined by Aristotle in his POETICS. Examples: Othello's jealousy and Hamlet's indecisiveness in OTHELLO (ca. 1604) and HAMLET (ca. 1601) respectively by William Shakespeare lead to the tragic *denouements*.

Harlem Renaissance [rɪ'neɪsns ☆ 'renəsɑ:ns]: a term used to describe the flowering of black art which took place in Harlem, New York, in the 1920s. The writers associated with this movement aimed to define and develop black culture, to protest against the oppressed status of blacks in American society and to make other blacks aware and proud of their heritage and culture. Among the writers associated with this movement are Langston Hughes and Countee Cullen.

hendiadys [hen'daɪədɪs] (n.): a stylistic device characterized by expressing one idea by two nouns linked by "and".
Examples: "darkness and the shadow of death"
"gloom and melancholy"

hero ['hɪərəʊ ☆ 'hi:-], fem. **heroine** ['herəʊɪn] (n.): the principal male or female *character* in a work of literature. The hero is usually in *conflict* with an opponent (*antagonist*), fate and/or society. The term *protagonist* is often used instead of hero, because hero has now come to signify a morally perfect person, while protagonist remains free from moral *connotations*; cf. *anti-hero*.

heroic couplet [hə,rəʊɪk 'kʌplɪt]: a pair of rhyming *iambic pentameters*. The second *line* is *end-stopped* to make the *couplet* a complete unit in itself. It was a very popular form in which to write *poems* from the 16th to the 19th centuries, although it had also been used earlier by Chaucer. It was occasionally used to end a *monologue* or a *scene* written in *blank verse* in a *drama*. Blank verse and heroic couplets differ only in the fact that the latter rhyme.
Examples: "The húngry júdges sóon the séntence sígn,
And wrétches háng that júry-mén may díne."
(Alexander Pope, "The Rape of the Lock", C, iii, 21; 1712)
"So cáll the fíelds to rést, and lét's awáy,
To párt the glóries óf this háppy dáy."
(William Shakespeare, JULIUS CAESAR, V, 80-81; ca. 1599)

hexameter [hek'sæmɪtə] (n.): a *metrical line* consisting of six feet (cf. *foot*). In English *poetry* it is rarely used and only with *iambic* feet (cf. *alexandrine*). The Greeks and Romans often used the *dactylic* hexameter.

homophone ['hɒməfəʊn ☆ 'hɑːm-] (n.): a word which is pronounced like another word, but which is spelled differently and has a different meaning; homophones are sometimes used in *poetry* to create *ambiguity*.
Example: "sun" and "son" are often used in religious poetry since both the sun and the son (of God) give light to the world.

hubris ['hjuːbrɪs] (n.): in *tragedy*, a term used to describe insolent pride. A tragic *hero's* hubris will cause him or her to ignore any kind of warning about the reckless path he or she is treading. This recklessness will eventually bring about his or her downfall. The term was coined by Aristotle in his POETICS.
Example: Caesar in William Shakespeare's JULIUS CAESAR (ca. 1599) refuses out of pride to heed the warnings he is given concerning his impending assassination.

humour ☆ **humor** ['hjuːmə], (n.) **humorous** (adj.): the quality of being entertaining or amusing. Humour may be achieved through various devices, e.g. wit, *puns*, *satire*, *slapstick*; not all forms of humour will be appreciated by every segment of society, since humour depends upon shared cultural values.

hyperbole [haɪ'pɜːbəlɪ] (n.): a figure of speech which contains an *exaggeration*. It is used to emphasize a particular feeling or longing, and may be used for either serious or *comic* effect.
Examples: I could eat a horse (i.e. eat a lot). Your suitcase weighs a ton (i.e. is very heavy). Both these hyperboles have now passed into the realm of *cliché*.

I

iamb ['aɪæmb] (n.), **iambic** [– ' – –] (adj.): a *metrical foot* of two syllables, the first unstressed and the second stressed: – ' – , e.g. decíde
It is the most common foot in English *verse*, being used in *blank verse* and *heroic couplets*.

identical rhyme [aɪ'dentɪkl]: the *repetition* of a word in the rhyming position for the purpose of emphasis.
Example: "Then all averred, I had killed the bird
That brought the fog and *mist*.
'Twas right, said they, such birds to stay,
That bring the fog and *mist*."
(Samuel Coleridge, "The Rime of the Ancient Mariner"; 1798)

idyll ['ɪdɪl ☆ 'aɪdl] (n.), **idyllic** [ɪ'dɪlɪk ☆ aɪ-] (adj.): originally a *poem* describing a scene in rural life, its meaning has now been extended to include any text or *episode* or event which describes a state of serenity, peace and tranquillity, especially a rural landscape.

image ['ɪmɪdʒ] (n.): a word or series of words used by a writer to appeal to the reader's imagination. An image is intended to bring a new feeling or perception to an object. The writer may appeal to any of the five senses or to the sense of movement to enable the reader to perceive an object. Many images are conveyed by *figurative* language, especially by *metaphors* and *similes*.

imagery ['ɪmɪdʒrɪ] (n.): a collective term for the use of *images* which seek to convey an impression of what the writer is describing.

Imagism ['ɪmɪdʒɪzm] (n.): a movement among English-speaking poets between 1910 and 1920 which sought to abandon poetic conventions and create new *rhythms*. The Imagist poets avoided long descriptions, but rather treated *images* with precision and concision. Commonplace subjects and ordinary language were used in the endeavour. Many Imagist poems are short and concise. The best-known Imagist poets are Ezra Pound and Amy Lowell.
Example: "The apparition of these faces in the crowd,
Petals on a wet, black bough."
(Ezra Pound, "In a Station of the Metro"; 1916)

imperfect rhyme: a *rhyme* in which the consonants of the rhymed word are the same or similar, but in which the vowels are different.

Example: "It seemed that out of battle I *escaped*
Down some profound dull tunnel, long since *scooped*
Through granites which titanic wars had *groined*.
Yet also there encumbered sleepers *groaned*"
(Wilfred Owen, "Strange Meeting"; 1918)

implicit characterization: a way of presenting a *character* indirectly. The reader or audience learns of the character through *dialogue* and *action*, rather than through *description*; cf. *explicit characterization*.

impressionistic description: the presentation of living beings, objects or processes based on the writer's or speaker's subjective impressions, so that the reader or listener receives only a suggestive mental picture of what is being described.

indirect characterization: cf. *implicit characterization*.

informal style [ɪnˈfɔːml] (adj.): the use of language by which a writer establishes a degree of familiarity between him or herself and the reader. It is intended to allow the reader to feel more comfortable and relaxed, as though he or she is intimate with the writer. Informal style is characterized by a personal, easy-going and subjective form of communication and by the frequent use of fairly simple, even slangy, vocabulary, short forms, uncomplicated sentence patterns and *ellipsis*; cf. *formal style, neutral style*.

instruction [– ' – –] (n.), **instructive** [– ' – –] (adj.): one of the five *text types*. An instructive text is intended to influence a reader's or listener's behaviour or actions by advising him or her about a particular matter. Characteristic of an instructive text is the use of commands and recommendations. *Didacticism* is a form of instruction, but is distinguishable in that the former deals with morality and aims to teach the reader or listener a lesson; often a didactic text can be merely *descriptive*, but from the description the reader is led to a certain conclusion concerning the moral behaviour of the *characters* presented. Instruction is more direct and need not deal with moral behaviour. Examples: The Ten Commandments in the Bible
A set of instructions on how to repair a puncture in a bike tyre
A recipe for a cake

intensifying adverb [ɪnˈtensɪfaɪŋ]: an adverb used to give more force to a statement, e.g. "indeed", "in fact", "particularly"; cf. *attitudinal adverb*.
Example: I am *particularly* fond of …

interior monologue [ɪnˈtɪərɪə]: a special kind of *scenic presentation*, in which a writer seeks to depict the thoughts or feelings passing through a *character's* mind. Often an interior monologue does not follow a *chronological order*, since, when people think, their thoughts jump from one subject to another without necessary logic. In this way the random flow of thought is presented to the reader or listener. It was very popular around the 1920s; cf. *stream of consciousness*.

Example: "God help the world if all the women were her sort down on bathing-suits and lownecks of course nobody wanted her to wear them I suppose she was pious because no man would look at her twice ..."

(James Joyce, ULYSSES; 1922)

interlude ['ıntəluːd] (n.): a short, entertaining piece of writing between two *acts* of a *drama*. They were popular in the Middle Ages and the Renaissance and were often of a *farcical* or *allegorical* nature.

internal conflict [ın'tɜːnl]: a struggle between two opposing views or values which takes place in a *character's* mind. Internal conflict is an important part

of *characterization*, since it reveals the character's motives, fears and desires. In *drama*, it is usually presented in the form of a *soliloquy*.

Example: "To be or not to be ..."

(William Shakespeare's HAMLET, III, i, 56–89; ca. 1601)

Here Hamlet displays his uncertainty as to whether or not he should avenge his father's death.

internal rhyme [ın'tɜːnl]: the rhyming of two or more words within a single *line* of *poetry*.

Example: "I am the *daughter* of Earth and *Water*,

And the nursling of the Sky;

I pass through the *pores* of the ocean and *shores*"

(Percy Shelley, "The Cloud"; 1820)

interpretive news story [ɪn'tɜːprɪtɪv ☆ -rət-]: a variant of the *text form report*. It is a journalistic report based on facts but including subjective, story-like elements. It usually stresses new developments and the course events will take in the future. The interpretation may be dubious, but it nevertheless helps the reader to get a broader view of the subject under discussion. An interpretive news story differs from a *feature story* in that it does not stress an individual's personal experience; it usually includes an analysis of facts, figures, developments, etc.

interview ['ɪntəvjuː] (n.): a *dialogue* in which somebody (usually a journalist) asks another person a series of questions, which are normally prepared in advance, about his or her life, opinions, etc. for publication or broadcast.

intrusive [ɪn'truːsɪv] (adj.): denoting a) an *author* who interposes occasional comments which draw attention to the fictional nature of the events – this is often used to achieve *estrangement* – or b) a *narrator* who comments on the *characters* and expresses his or her views about the events or about human life. It is sometimes difficult to differentiate between an intrusive *omniscient narrator* and an intrusive author.
Example: "I wish some well-fed philosopher, whose meat and drink turn to
gall within him, ... could have seen Oliver Twist clutching at the
dainty viands that the dog had neglected."
(Charles Dickens, OLIVER TWIST; 1837–1838)

invective [ɪn'vektɪv] (n.): a *speech* or piece of writing intended to attack, denounce or abuse somebody or something. It can also be used for a humorous effect if the insults are overblown and ridiculous.
Example: "OSWALD: What dost thou know me for?
KENT: A knave, a rascal, an eater of broken meats; a base, proud,
shallow, beggarly, three-suited, hundred-pound, filthy, worsted-
stocking knave ..."
(William Shakespeare, KING LEAR, II, ii, 13–16; ca. 1605)

irony ['aɪrənɪ] (n.), **ironic(al)** [aɪ'rɒnɪk(l) ☆-'rɑː-] (adj.): there are various kinds of irony:
Verbal irony is the use of words to express the opposite of the words' *literal* meaning. The writer or speaker says something he or she does not actually mean; the reader or audience understands the irony through the *tone* in which the words are expressed or through shared cultural values.
Structural or situational irony is the *contrast* between what the *narrator* or speaker wants and what he or she actually gets. Such irony is normally maintained throughout a text, and can be projected through a naive narrator who interprets events or reveals his or her ambitions in such a way that the reader is aware of the narrator's shortcomings but the narrator him or herself

is not. Another form of structural irony is achieved by a writer adopting another person's *point of view* for the purpose of ridiculing it; the writer expresses belief in something but denounces it through his or her choice of words or tone; cf. *dramatic irony, tragic irony, sarcasm.*

Examples: (verbal irony) In William Shakespeare's JULIUS CAESAR (ca. 1599) Anthony uses irony in his *speech* beginning "Friends, Romans, Countrymen" (III, ii, 75–254), when he continually repeats the word "honourable" when describing the conspirators against Caesar; in fact he means quite the opposite.

(structural irony) In William Shakespeare's HAMLET (ca. 1601) Rosencrantz and Guildenstern travel to England with orders to murder Hamlet; it is they, however, who end up being killed.

J

Jacobean [dʒækə'biːən] (adj.): pertaining to the reign of James I (1603–1625). These years were marked by a wealth of literature. William Shakespeare, Ben Jonson and John Donne all wrote their best work during this period. The King James (or Authorized Version) Bible was also published during the reign of James I.

journal ['dʒɜːnl] (n.): a daily record of events. It is usually less personal than a *diary*. The term may also be used to refer to a magazine or *review*, which deals with academic subjects.

K

keyword outline [,– – '– –]: A type of *outline* which presents the main ideas of a text in the form of key words and phrases.

kitchen-sink drama [,– – – '– –]: a kind of *drama* which shows aspects of working-class life in a realistic fashion. Normally the drama centres around the kitchen of a working-class family, since it is the room where the family members eat, drink and talk. The term became popular in the 1950s when it was used, often derogatorily, to refer to the plays of writers such as John Osborne and Arnold Wesker. Kitchen-sink drama represented a move away from the pleasant *settings* of middle-class drawing rooms of previous decades.
Example: Arnold Wesker, CHICKEN SOUP TRILOGY (1960)

L

Lake Poets: a term used to refer to the *Romantic* poets William Wordsworth, Samuel Coleridge and Robert Southey, who settled around 1800 in the Lake District in northern England.

lament [lə'ment] (n.): a *poem* of mourning for a person or because of a *tragic* event.

layout ['leɪaʊt] (n.): the choice of letters, print and general arrangement of written and/or pictorial material on the page of a book, newspaper, magazine, etc. The layout determines the readability and attractiveness of a printed text, and is also used to highlight or emphasize certain parts of the text.

leader ['liːdə] (n.) (BE): cf. *editorial*.

leading article [,– – '– – –] (BE): cf. *editorial*.

legend ['ledʒənd] (n.): a story which lies between *myth* and historical fact; it originally referred to the story of a saint's life. A legend usually concerns a *character* (who may or may not have existed) and describes various adventures or episodes from his or her life. If the character is a real-life historical figure, apocryphal stories are often attributed to him or her. Legends form part of the oral tradition of most cultures.

leitmotif ['laɪtməʊˌtiːf] (n.): a term derived from music denoting a *theme*, expression or object which recurs throughout a text; it is intentionally employed by a writer to refer to a person, situation or *atmosphere* and to help give structure to a text.

letter to the editor ['edɪtə]: a letter written by a reader of a newspaper or magazine to its editor in order to express a personal opinion on some topic of general interest or to react to an article which previously appeared in that newspaper or magazine. It is written with the intention of being published by the newspaper or magazine and read by other readers. The subject may vary from politics to bird-watching. The letter to the editor is a variant of the *text form comment*.

limerick ['lɪmərɪk] (n.): a kind of light *verse*. It consists of 5 predominantly *anapaestic lines* with the *rhyme scheme* a a b b a. The limerick became popular in the 19th century; it is usually witty, sometimes sophisticated or *grotesque* and occasionally obscene. It often contains a surprising final line.

Example: "In a nótable fámily called Stéin
There's Gértrude, there's Ép, and there's Éin.
Gert's wríting is házy,
Ep's státues are crázy,
And nóbody únderstands Éin."

limited point of view: the *narration* of a *fictional* text from the *point of view* of only a few, or just one, of the *characters* in the text. The *narrator* describes only the thoughts and experiences of those characters, who then become the focus of the narration. The reader thereby senses his or her participation in the *action* by following closely only the experiences of these characters. A *first person narrator* always has a limited point of view.

line (n.): a structural unit in a *poem*; it is usually classified by the number of feet it contains. Most lines contain between 3 and 8 feet.

listing order ['lɪstɪŋ]: a way of structuring a text by enumerating its items. The order in which they are listed is not necessarily dependent on the items' importance; usually the items are numbered or introduced by adverbs like "first", "then" and "finally".

literal (adj.): language used according to its original meaning, as contrasted with *figurative* meaning.

litotes [laɪ'təʊtiːz] (n.): an *understatement* usually used in *irony*. Usually an affirmation is expressed by the negative of the contrary; cf. *meiosis*.
Example: "He's not bright", when "he's stupid" is meant.

Liverpool poets: a group of poets living in Liverpool in the early 1960s. They wrote popular *poetry*, using everyday speech, and gave public recitals of their poetry. The prinicipal poets are Adrian Henri, Roger McGough and Brian Patten.

local colour ☆ **color** [,– – '– –]: a term applied to writing in which the region or area a story is set in plays an important role. The writer attempts to bring out the *atmosphere* of the region through the description of the landscape, lifestyle, customs, etc. which set it apart from other regions.
Examples: Thomas Hardy's novels reflect life in the south-west of England.
Mark Twain's HUCKLEBERRY FINN (1884) describes life on the Mississippi River.

low comedy: a kind of *comedy* which bases its *humour* on coarse and often bawdy jokes, and makes use of *slapstick* and ridicule. It appeals more to instinct than to intellect. Low comedy may be used to refer to *comic relief* in *drama*, especially in Renaissance drama, where it was particularly popular, or to any bawdy *episode* in a work of literature.

lyric ['lırık] (n.), **lyrical** ['– – –] (adj.): a *poem* which expresses the personal thoughts and feelings of a single *speaker*. The speaker is not necessarily identical to the poet. Love, religious fervour, metaphysical anguish and lamentation are popular subjects in lyrics. A lyric tends to be short and may be written in almost any variety of poetical form, with *sonnets*, *odes* and *elegies* being the most popular forms. The term lyrical may also be applied to personal, subjective and sensual passages in a *prose* work. Lyric was one of the three Greek *genres*.

lyrics ['lırıks] (pl.): the words of a song, especially a pop song.

M

malapropism: the deliberate misuse of a word for *humorous* purposes. The term derives from Mrs Malaprop in Richard Sheridan's THE RIVALS (1775), who used long words incorrectly in an attempt to sound learned. However, malapropisms existed long before the name was coined.
Examples: "MRS MALAPROP: Illiterate him, I say, quite from your memory."
(Richard Sheridan, THE RIVALS, I, ii; 1775)
Here she means "eliminate".
"DOGBERRY: Comparisons are odorous"
(William Shakespeare, MUCH ADO ABOUT NOTHING, III, v, 15; ca. 1598)
Here he means "odious".

masculine rhyme ['mæskjʊlɪn]: a *rhyme* of one stressed syllable.
Examples: bright/light; wood/stood.

meiosis [maɪ'əʊsɪs] (n.): an *understatement*, usually expressed through saying that something is less in quality, size, etc. than it actually is; cf. *litotes*.
Example: "This wine is rather good", when "very good" is meant.

melodrama ['melə,drɑːmə] (n.): a type of *drama* characterized by the use of sensationalism and sentimentalism. The *characters* are usually superficially portrayed and display strong emotions. Melodrama was particularly popular in the 19th century.

memoirs ['memwɑːz] (pl., n.): a *narrative* text which contains an account of various episodes in the writer's life. Memoirs and *autobiography* are often interchangeable terms; memoirs refer mainly to a limited area of experiences, e.g. a writer's political life, travels, etc., whereas an autobiography usually deals with the writer's entire life or clearly limited periods of his or her life.

metaphor ['metəfə ☆ -fɔːr] (n.), **metaphorical** [,– – '– – –] (adj.): a stylistic device in which two seemingly unlike things are linked with one another in the form of an implicit comparison. The strength of a metaphor lies in its ability to convey a new and quite different feeling and meaning to the *denotation* of a word. Metaphor differs from *simile* in that metaphor says something is something else, whereas a simile says something is like something else.
Examples: "There's daggers in men's smiles."
(William Shakespeare, MACBETH, II, iii, 147; ca. 1606)
"Now I seemed landed in a safe harbour after the stormy voyage of life past was at an end."
(Daniel Defoe, MOLL FLANDERS; 1722)

"In the midst of this chopping sea of civilized life, such are the clouds and storms and quicksands and thousand-and-one items to be allowed for, that a man has to live, if he would not founder and go to the bottom and not make his port at all, by dead reckoning, and he must be a great calculator indeed who succeeds."
(Henry Thoreau, WALDEN; 1854)

Metaphysical poets [ˌmetə'fɪzɪkl]: a term applied to a group of 17th-century English poets. Living at quite separate times and writing about quite distinct *themes* and with different beliefs, their *poetry* is characterized by complex *imagery, conceits* and *metaphors*. The term "metaphysical" is misleading, since few of the Metaphysical poets wrote about metaphysics or religion; the term was applied to them because they expressed difficult thoughts in a concentrated *style*. The leading Metaphysical poets were John Donne, George Herbert and Andrew Marvell.

metonomy [me'tɒnɪmɪ] (n.): a figure of speech in which the name of an attribute of an object or of a thing associated with the object is substituted for the object itself; cf. *synecdoche*.

The pen is mightier than the sword.

Examples: "Sword" can be used as a metonomy for "military might".
"The White House" can be used as a metonomy for "the American government".

metre ☆ **meter** ['miːtə] (n.), **metric/al** (adj.): the regular *rhythmic* patterns of a *poem*, i.e. the arrangement of words according to stressed and unstressed syllables. Each *line* of a poem is divided into metrical feet (cf. *foot*), although modern *poetry* often avoids the use of traditional metre. The number of feet per line varies with each poem and can vary within a poem.

The most common metres are the *pentameter* (with 5 feet) and the *hexameter* (with 6 feet). The natural rhythm of speech often conflicts with the metre of a poem.

mixed metaphor [‚– '– – –]: a combination of two *metaphors* which are incongruous; it is often intentionally used to achieve a *humorous* effect.
Examples: "It seems we'll just have to grit our teeth and bite the bullet."
(Jonathan Lynn, Antony Jay, YES, PRIME MINISTER; 1986)
"To take up arms against a sea of troubles"
(William Shakespeare, HAMLET, III, i, 59; ca. 1601)

mock epic [‚– '– –]: a *narrative poem* which deals with a trivial subject in an elevated manner. Mock epic is a form of *burlesque* which ridicules or *satirizes* a certain subject matter. The *style* of the mock epic is usually referred to as "mock-heroic".
Example: Alexander Pope's THE RAPE OF THE LOCK (1712), which deals with a young suitor cutting off a young lady's lock of hair. Pope describes the event and the ensuing row between the two families as though they were matters of great importance.

mode of presentation [‚– – – – '– –]: the way of relating a story. The *author* (or the *narrator*) can either tell the reader about events and their significance (*panoramic presentation*) or show the reader what is happening (*scenic presentation*). Usually a combination of both are used in a *narrative*. The mode of presentation is a means of influencing the reader's reactions and highlighting parts of the narrative. The relationship between *acting time* and *narrating time* is dependent upon the mode of presentation.

monodrama ['mɒnəʊ,drɑːmə] (n.): a *drama* in which there is only one *character*. It is therefore a kind of *monologue*, in which the character may either express his or her particular thoughts or talk to imaginary characters on the stage.
Example: Willy Russell, SHIRLEY VALENTINE (1988)

monologue ['mɒnəlɒg ☆ 'mɑːnəlɔːg](n.): an extended *speech* by a *character* in any form of *fictional* text. A monologue may be an address to other characters in the text or to the reader or listener, or it may be the expression of the thoughts of the character, e.g. in a *soliloquy*.
Examples: "Friends, Romans, Countrymen …"
(Mark Anthony's speech in William Shakespeare's JULIUS CAESAR, III, ii, 75–109; ca. 1599)
"To be or not to be …"
(Hamlet's speech in William Shakespeare's HAMLET, III, i, 56–89; ca. 1601)

moral ['mɒrəl] (n.): the lesson contained or taught by a text; it may be expressed explicitly in a final statement, as is often the case in *fables*, or implicitly through the *plot*.

motif [məʊ'tiːf] (n.): a dominant idea recurring through a literary text. It may be a *character*, an event, an *image* or a sentence. Motifs are used to give unity to a text and to express, without going into its explanation, a particular *atmosphere* which is associated with the motif.

Movement, the: a term used to describe a group of writers (especially poets) in the 1950s who used rational intelligence and fine craftmanship in their writings; their works are characterized by understatement and wit. Among those associated with the Movement are Philip Larkin, Kingsley Amis and John Wain.

myth [mɪθ] (n.), **mythical** ['mɪθɪkl] (adj.): an ancient story dealing with supernatural beings and *heroes* and heroines. Myths relate the formation or creation of geographical phenomena or of certain human feelings and concepts. Myths can be considered *archetypal*, since they are usually expressions of subconscious experiences shared by all human beings.

N

narrating time [nə'reɪtɪŋ ☆ 'næ-]: the time it takes to relate a particular *episode* or events in a *narrative* text. The narrating time is dependent upon the *mode of presentation* and is the same as *reading time*; cf. *acting time*.

narration [nə'reɪʃn] (n.), **narrative** ['nærətɪv] (adj.; also n.): one of the five *text types*; it presents actions or events in some kind of logical *temporal order*. These actions or events are interrelated and follow on one from another. Most *fictional* texts, e.g. novels and short stories, belong to the text type narration. Narrative (also known as *epic*) was one of the original three Greek *genres*.

narrative verse [ˌnærətɪv 'vɜːs]: *poetry* or a *poem* that tells a story. Usually it is relatively long poem and deals with an elevated subject; cf. *ballad*, *epic*.
Examples: John Milton's PARADISE LOST (1658–1663)
　　　　　　Wilfred Owen, "Strange Meeting" (1918)
　　　　　　E.A. Poe, "The Raven" (1845)

narrator [nə'reɪtə ☆ 'næ-] (n.): the person who tells the story in a *narrative* text. There are various types of narrator:
a) *first-person narrator*. A first-person narrator may be i) a *dramatized narrator*, e.g. the *protagonist* of the text or a secondary *character* (witness/observer narrator), with a *limited point of view*, or ii) an *intrusive author* or narrator, who comments on the *action* from outside the text, with an *unlimited point of view*.
b) *third-person narrator*. A third-person narrator may be either i) an *omniscient narrator*, in that he or she tells the story from different angles and perspectives and has an unlimited point of view, or ii) a character in the story, with a limited point of view.
The narrator may either be intrusive, commenting on the story, or objective, giving no opinion of his or her own. The narrator may be reliable (when the reader is able to take everything the narrator tells at face value), unreliable (when the reader must construe for him or herself just how much of the narrator's story is reliable) or self-conscious (i.e. interrupting to discuss the problems involved in narrating). The narrator of a text is rarely to be identified with the *author*; cf. *speaker*.

Naturalism ['nætʃrəlɪzm] (n.): a movement in literature between 1860 and 1900, which sought to present human life as being entirely dictated by natural laws. Naturalist writers refused to idealize human experience; they were meticulous in their portrayal of society, concentrating particularly on the middle and working classes. Although Naturalism was primarily a French and German movement, it influenced several American writers, e.g. Stephen Crane and Theodore Dreiser.

Neoclassicism (n.), **Neoclassical** (adj.): a term used to refer to the period between ca. 1660 and 1800, when British writers derived their inspiration from the ancient Classical writers of Greece and Rome. Among the writers of this time were John Dryden, Alexander Pope and Samuel Johnson; cf. *Enlightenment, Classicism.*

neutral style ['njuːtrəl ☆ 'nuːtr-]: language distinguished by a choice of words and sentence structure that make it appropriate to any situation or *text form*. It is normal, educated written *style*, between *formal style*, which is used mostly in official publications, and *informal style*, which is used mostly in colloquial texts.

news story [njuːz ☆ nuːz]: a variant of the *text form report*; it is based on facts, enriched by background information and deals with an event that is topical and of interest to a sizeable section of the general public.

non-fiction [,– '– –] (n.): a category of texts that deals with facts, real events, people, etc. *Comments, biographies* and *reports* are examples of *non-fictional* texts; cf. *fiction.*

nonsense verse [,– – '–]: a type of *poetry* which has a simple *rhythm* and *rhyme scheme* and deals with an absurd topic in an illogical way. The term is derived from Edward Lear's BOOK OF NONSENSE (1846).
Example: "Far and few, far and few,
      Are the lands where the Jumblies live;
      Their heads are green, and their hands are blue,
      And they went to sea in a Sieve."
      (Edward Lear, "The Jumblies"; 1846)

novel ['nɒvl ☆ 'nɑːvl] (n.): a long and complex *fictional narrative* text written in *prose*. It contains *characters, action* and, usually, *plot*. Novels are extremely varied in *style, form* and content. The novel became fully established in the 18th century in Britain.

novelette [,nɒvə'let ☆ ,nɑːv-] (n.): a *fictional* text written in *prose* which is shorter than a *novel* but longer than a *short story*. It is often used derogatorily to signify popular fiction with no literary merit; cf. *novella.*

novella [nəʊ'velə] (n.): the term for any *fictional* text written in *prose* which is shorter than a *novel* but longer than a *short story*; cf. *novelette.*
Example: Ernest Hemingway, THE OLD MAN AND THE SEA (1952)

nursery rhyme ['nɜːsərɪ]: a *verse* or verses sung or recited by children or by parents to their children. Nursery rhymes belong to the oral tradition and go back far in history. The *lyrics* often refer to historical events.

Example: "Ring a ring o'roses
A pocket full of posies
A-tishoo! A-tishoo!
We all fall down."
This nursery rhyme refers to the bubonic plague.

O

octet: cf. *octave*.

octave ['ɒktɪv ☆ 'ɑːkt-] (n.): a group of eight rhyming *lines*, either as the first unit of a Petrarchan *sonnet*, usually with the *rhyme scheme* a b b a a b b a, or as a complete *stanza* rhyming a b a b a b c c. An octave can also be referred to as an "octet".

ode [əʊd] (n.): a long *lyric poem* often with an elaborate *stanza* structure and a *formal style* and solemn *tone*. Odes are usually poems of praise directed towards somebody or something.
Example: "Thou wast not born for death, immortal Bird!
        No hungry generations tread thee down;
        The voice I hear this passing night was heard
        In ancient days by emperor and clown."
(John Keats, "Ode to a Nightingale"; 1819)

omniscient narrator [ɒm'nɪsɪənt ☆ ɑːm'nɪʃnt]: a *narrator* in a text who appears to know everything about the *characters*, including their thoughts and feelings, and events in the story being told. An omniscient narrator relates from an *unlimited point of view*, although, in actual fact, only certain things are revealed to the reader, and often character judgments are of a superficial nature. Omniscient narrators often reveal in an objective way such information as they consider necessary for the reader to understand the *action* of the events.

one-act play [,–– '–]: a short *drama* consisting of only one *act*. It usually deals with one single *episode* or event involving a limited number of *characters*. Its shortness prevents much character or *plot* development.
It became popular in the 20th century.
Example: Alan Ayckbourn, A TALK IN
      THE PARK (1974)

onomatopeia [,ɒnəʊmætə'piːə ☆ ,ɑːnə-]
(n.), **onomatopoeic** [,ɒnəʊmætə'piːɪk]
☆ **onomatopoetic** [,––––– '––](adj.):
a figure of speech characterized by the
use of words which imitate the sounds
they refer to, e.g. "buzz", "cuckoo". It
may also be used to apply to a group
of words which evoke a feeling of

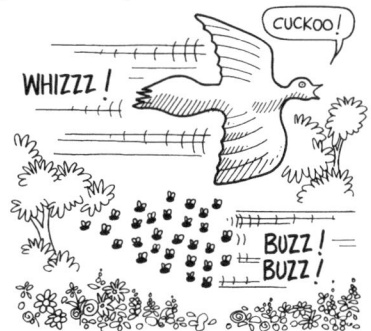

The cuckoo whizzed past the buzzing bees.

sound, mood or movement; *assonance* and *alliteration* are often used to achieve this effect.

Examples: "The whole house ... echoed with *squeaks* and *twills* of the instruments and with the *buzz* and *hum* of voices."
(Virginia Woolf, THE YEARS; 1937)
"Only the *stuttering rifles's rapid rattle*
Can *patter out* their hasty orisons."
(Wilfred Owen, "Anthem for Doomed Youth"; 1917)

open ending [,– – '– –]: a structural element of a *fictional* text in which the *conflict* remains for the most part unresolved and there is no final *denouement*. Open endings are common in literature, because they are held to be a reflection of real life, which lacks neat, easy solutions. Often they allow the reader to decide how the text would proceed if it continued; cf. *plot*.

Example: John Fowles's THE FRENCH LIEUTENANT'S WOMAN (1969), in which two possible endings are offered to the reader.

order ['ɔːdə] (n.): the general structure of a text; cf. *chronological order, climactic order, contrastive order, dialectical order, listing order, temporal order, topical order*.

outline ['aʊtlaɪn]: a *text form* belonging to the *text type exposition*; it contains a systematic, condensed arrangement of important information from a text. It presents the main ideas of the paragraph or text, their supporting ideas and, often, important details, in a visually structured format so that the important points are quickly identifiable; cf. *keyword outline*.

oxymoron [ˌɒksɪˈmɔːrɒn ☆ ,ɑːksɪˈmɔːrɑːn] (n.): a stylistic device characterized by the combination of two or more incongruous or openly contradictory words and meanings; it is often used to depict indecision or torment; cf. *paradox*.

Examples: "Alas! that love, whose view is muffled still
should, *without eyes, see* pathways to his will ...
Here's much to do with hate, but more with love:
Why then, O *branding love*! O *loving hate*!"
(William Shakespeare, ROMEO AND JULIET; I, ii, 177–181; ca. 1595)
"... I *burn* and *freeze* like ice"
(Sir Thomas Wyatt, "I Find No Peace")

P

palindrome ['pælɪndrəʊm] (n.): a word or sentence which reads the same forwards and backwards.
Examples: civic
Madam, I'm Adam
a man, a plan, a canal, Panama!

pamphlet ['pæmflɪt] (n.): a small, unbound printed book, usually with paper covers, which is mainly used by writers to express their political or religious views.

panegyric [ˌpænə'dʒɪrɪk ☆ -'dʒaɪr-]: cf. *eulogy*.

panoramic presentation [ˌpænə'ræmɪk]: a *mode of presentation* in which a story or part of a story is told as a condensed series of events. It provides an opportunity for the *writer* to convey information in a relatively short period of time; cf. *scenic presentation*.

pantomime ['pæntəmaɪm] (n.): a type of *drama* for children which is usually based on a *fairy tale*. It includes music and songs, and there is usually audience participation. The principal male *character* and at least one lady (usually a *comic*, ugly or older character) are played by members of the opposite sex. Pantomime is a particularly British form of entertainment, and is staged around Christmas.

parable ['pærəbl] (n.): a short *fictional narrative* text which makes a general statement about existence or teaches a moral or religious lesson. The *moral* of a parable is rarely explicitly stated; rather, the reader or listener is expected to draw a parallel between the story and his or her own experience. A parable is *allegorical* in that it can be understood at two levels: factual and spiritual. A parable differs from a *fable* in that a parable uses humans rather than animals and the stories are simpler and less ingenious.
The most famous parables are those of Christ, which are related in the Bible; they involve an exploration of the relationship between God and humanity, and between individuals. Modern parables tend to involve examination of human existence.
Examples: Christ's "The Good Samaritan"
John Rae's "Parable of the Good Lunatic" (1978)

paradox ['pærədɒks ☆ -dɑːks] (n.), **paradoxical** [ˌ-- '---] (adj.): a statement that seems to be self-contradictory, but which may contain some truth; cf. *oxymoron*.

Examples: "Cowards die many times before their deaths"
(William Shakespeare, JULIUS CAESAR, II, ii, 33; ca. 1599)
"cries she / with silent lips"
(Emma Lazarus, "The New Colossus"; 1883)

parallelism ['pærəlelɪzm] (n.): the *repetition* of the same or similar syntactical form in different sentences or parts of the same sentence; cf. *anaphora*.
Example: *"Cursed be the social wants that sin against the strength of youth!*
Cursed be the social lies that warp us from the living truth!
Cursed be the sickly forms that err from honest nature's rule!"
(Alfred, Lord Tennyson, "Locksley Hall"; 1837–1838)

paraphrase ['pærəfreɪz] (n.): a restatement of a text in other words, in order to simplify, clarify or reinterpret the original text.

parody ['pærədɪ] (n.): a *fictional* text which imitates certain elements of another well-known piece of writing in order to make the original appear ridiculous.

pathetic fallacy [pə,θetɪk 'fæləsɪ]: the reflection of a *character's* or *speaker's* mood onto nature or the attribution of human feelings to inanimate objects or animals. It differs from *personification* in that it involves human emotions being reflected in nature, whereas personification makes the objects or animals into humans. The term was coined by John Ruskin in MODERN PAINTERS (1856).

Example: "Out of the smudgy little window you could see an immense expanse of *sad-looking* sky, and whenever there were clouds they looked *very worn, old clouds, frayed at the edges, with holes in them, or dark stains like tea.*"
(Katherine Mansfield, "Life of Ma Parker"; 1922)

pathos ['peɪθɒs ☆ -ɑːs] (n.): the evocation of strong feelings of pity, sympathy, sorrows or tenderness.

pattern poem: cf. *concrete poem*.

pentameter [pen'tæmɪtə] (n.): a *line* consisting of five feet (cf. *foot*). It is the most popular *metre* in English *poetry*, as *blank verse, sonnets* and *heroic couplets* are all written in *iambic* pentameters.
Example: "When to | the ses|sions of | sweet si|lent thought"
(William Shakespeare, "Sonnet 30"; 1593–1600)

perfect rhyme: cf. *pure rhyme*.

peripeteia [ˌperɪpə'tiːə] (n.), also **peripety** [pə'rɪpəti] (n.): the reversal of the *protagonist's* fortune from prosperity to ruin. This occurs because the protagonist acts in a way which is inappropriate to his or her circumstances or when the outcome of the protagonist's actions is the opposite of what he or she intended. It may also be brought about by another *character* who wishes him or her well, but unwittingly destroys him or her.

periphrasis [pə'rɪfrəsɪs] (n.), pl. **periphrases** [pə'rɪfrəsiːz]: a roundabout wayof speaking or writing, usually through the use of long, unclear phrasesand expressions to convey a message that could be more clearly andsimply related. Periphrasis is often found in bureaucratic language.

personification [pɜːsɒnɪfɪ'keɪʃn ☆ -ˌsɑːn-] (n.), **personify** [– '– – –] (v.): the technique of representing animals, plants, objects, or abstract ideas as if they were human beings and possessed human qualities.
Example: "The moping owl does to the moon complain" (Thomas Gray, "Elegy Written in a Country Churchyard"; 1751)

The moping owl does to the moon complain.

plagiarism ['pleɪdʒərɪzm] (n.): the use of one writer's words by another writer as though they were his or her own. Plagiarism is a derogatory term; it implies that the imitator is second-rate and is using the original writer's material for quick profit. Imitation and borrowing, on the other hand, belong to literary tradition; cf. *allusion*.

play [pleɪ] (n.): any dramatic work intended to be presented on stage, in film or on television.

pleonasm ['pliːənæzm] (n.), **pleonastic** [ˌpliːə'næstɪk] (adj.): the use of unnecessary and superfluous words; it is usually found in speech; cf. *tautology*.
Example: each of the *two* twins

plot [plɒt ☆ plɑːt] (n.): in *fictional* texts, the *action* structured as a set of events connected by cause and effect and centred around one or more *conflicts*. Plot is traditionally composed of the following elements, usually in this order: *exposition, rising action, climax, turning point, falling action, denouement* (or *open ending*). Plot creates *suspense* in a text, whereas *characters* and *descriptions* provide interest. E.M. Forster described plot in these terms: " 'The king died and then the queen died', is a story. 'The king died and then the queen died of grief', is a plot." (ASPECTS OF THE NOVEL; 1927) Some modern writers have attempted to write stories which lack plot.

poem ['pəʊɪm] (n.): a unified and independent composition, which contains a structured *line* sequence and is characterized by a special arrangement of words which produces a stylized *rhythm*. Poems vary greatly in *theme, atmosphere* and structure. Traditional poems use *metres* and feet (cf. *foot*) to achieve rhythm and almost always contain rhyming words at the end of the lines; modern *poetry* tends to use *free verse*, which produces different sorts of rhythm. A poem may be divided into *stanzas*; it may be *lyrical, epic* or *narrative*. A marked feature of most poems is the use of rich *imagery* in order to transform the world of the reader.

poet laureate [ˌpəʊɪt 'lɔːrɪət]: the title given to a poet who becomes an officer of the British Royal Household. Originally the duties involved writing *poetry* on state or royal occasions. The post is held for life. Poets laureate have included William Wordsworth, Alfred Tennyson and Ted Hughes. Since 1985 the USA has also had poet laureates; they are appointed for one year only.

poetic diction [pəʊˌetɪk 'dɪkʃn]: the language used by a writer, especially by a poet. Poetic diction refers to the choice and arrangement of words in writing that makes the writing individual, unique, original and imaginative, and separates it from normal language. The term poetic diction is also often used to describe 18th-century poetic language, which became overelaborate and sophisticated.

poetic justice [pəʊˌetɪk 'dʒʌstɪs]: in a *fictional* text, the concept that good should be rewarded and evil punished. This is the concept on which most moral and *didactic* literature is based.

Example: In William Shakespeare's MEASURE FOR MEASURE (ca. 1604) poetic justice is seen to be at work when the hypocritical and cruel Angelo is condemned to death and the virtuous Isabella is rewarded through marriage to the Duke.

poetry ['pəʊɪtrɪ] (n.): a term used to refer to literature that is not *prose*, i.e. that has some pattern based on *rhyme*, sentence structure and/or *metre*.

point of view [,– – '–]: the perspective from which the *characters*, topics and events are presented. The point of view establishes the relationship between the reader and the text. It may be limited, i.e. the *action*, etc. are approached from one particular angle, or unlimited, i.e. the reader can examine the action and characters from various angles (cf. *omniscient narrator*). The point of view is dependent on the *narrator*.

précis ['preɪsiː ☆ – '–] (n., also pl.): cf. *summary*.

prologue ['prəʊlɒg ☆ -lɔːg]: the opening section of a literary work, in which the subject or theme of the work is introduced.
Example: The "General Prologue" to Geoffrey Chaucer's THE CANTERBURY TALES (1387–1400)

prose [prəʊz] (n. & adj.): the term used to describe all writing which is not *poetry*, i.e. without *rhyme*, limited sentence structure and *metre*. Prose may be unadorned and use the form and words of ordinary language, or it may be elaborate, *rhythmic* and full of *imagery*.

prose poem [,prəʊz 'pəʊɪm]: a type of short and compact *prose* work which through its *poetic diction*, internal *rhythm* and *imagery* gives the feeling of being a *poem*. Like a poem it is a concise and unified text. It is more often than not *lyrical* rather than *narrative*. Prose poems were particularly popular in 19th-century France.

protagonist [prəʊ'tægənɪst] (n.): the main *character* in a *fictional* text, especially a *drama*. A protagonist may be either good or bad and is usually in *conflict* with an *antagonist*; cf. *hero*.

proverb ['prɒvɜːb ☆ 'prɑːv-] (n.): a concise saying which embodies a general truth. Proverbs differ from *aphorisms* in that they are usually of great antiquity and have their origins in oral tradition. "Adage" is a synonym of "proverb".
Example: Too many cooks spoil the broth.

pun [pʌn] (n.): a figure of speech which involves a play on words, in which one word has two different meanings, so that a sentence can be understood in two different ways. Puns are usually used for *humorous* effect.

Examples: "MERCUTIO: [...] Ask for me tomorrow, and you shall find me a grave man."
(William Shakespeare, ROMEO AND JULIET, III, i, 100–101; ca. 1595)
Here Mercutio has been mortally wounded and knows he will die.
"John Donne, Anne Donne, Un-done"
The poet John Donne wrote these lines to his wife Anne after their marriage. His father-in-law's opposition to the marriage resulted in John Donne's removal from office.

pure rhyme [pjʊə]: a *rhyme* with a perfect identity of sounds. It is also referred to as a "perfect rhyme".
Example: men/hen

Q

quatrain ['kwɒtreɪn ☆ 'kwɑːtr-] (n.): a *stanza* of four *lines*; cf. *sonnet*.

quintain ['kwɪntɪn] (n.): a *stanza* of five *lines*.

quintet [kwɪn'tet]: cf. *quintain*.

R

reading time ['– – –]: the time it takes to read about an event or series of events in a literary text. Reading time is usually the same as *narrating time*, but is almost always shorter than *acting time*, because in several minutes one can read of the passing of years.

realism ['rɪəlɪzm] (n.): a term used to describe art and literature which attempt to reflect life without idealization. Realistic literature often depicts the day-to-day life of ordinary people, in which there are no great adventures or *conflicts*. More specifically realism may be used to describe a movement in French literature in the 19th century which laid emphasis on the close attention to detail and facts.

recoil ['riːkɔɪl] (n.): in *tragedy*, a term used to indicate that the *protagonist* has brought about his or her own downfall.

refrain [rə'freɪn] (n.): a *line* or lines repeated at various intervals throughout a *poem*. Refrains normally occur at the end of a *stanza*. In *sea shanties* and other songs the refrain is normally called the *chorus*.
    Example: In Dylan Thomas's poem "Do not go gentle into that good night" (1946) the two lines "Old age should burn and rave at close of day" and "Rage, rage against the dying of the light" act as alternating refrains throughout the poem.

repartee [ˌrepɑː'tiː] (n.): a quick and witty reply to another person's remarks, often with a *sarcastic* undertone.
    Example: Lady to Churchill: "Churchill, if you were my husband, I would put poison in your tea."
    Churchill to lady: "Lady, if I were your husband, I would drink it."

repetition [ˌrepɪ'tɪʃn] (n.): the repeated use of particular sounds, syllables, words, phrases, sentences, etc. in order to structure a text and achieve a particular effect. *Parallelism* and *anaphora* are both types of repetition.

report [rɪ'pɔːt] (n.): a *non-fictional text form* belonging to the *text type narration*. It provides answers to the questions "who?", "what?", "when?", "where?" and "why?" – the so-called *five w's* –, which can be checked and verified by the reader or listener. Included under the term report are *news stories*, *feature stories*, histories and *biographies*.

reportage [ˌrɪˈpɔːˈtɑːʒ]: technique in which an *author* incorporates some personal, and usually newsworthy, experience into a *fictional* work.
  Example: In *The Quiet American* (1955) Graham Greene reproduces word for word an actual press conference which he attended.

Restoration comedy [ˌrestəˈreɪʃn]: a type of *comedy* that became popular following the restoration of the English monarchy in 1660; such comedies remained popular until the Hanoverian succession in 1714. During the *Commonwealth period* (1649–60) theatres had been closed and the country had been ruled over by a religious, middle-class dictatorship. Restoration comedy represents a reaction against puritan values; these comedies concerned sexual and marital intrigues, had aristocratic protagonists, witty *dialogue* and artificial *plots*. Most of the Restoration comedies are *comedies of manners*.
  Examples: Sir George Etherege, SHE WOULD IF SHE COULD (1668)
       William Congreve, LOVE FOR LOVE (1695)

revenge tragedy [rɪˈvendʒ]: a form of *tragedy* which deals with revenge or the righting of a wrong. Revenge tragedies may involve either a *hero* or *villain* seeking revenge; they were very popular in England between 1580 and 1630. They could provide a vehicle for examining moral *conflicts* or merely be a way of entertaining an audience by littering the stage with bodies.
  Examples: William Shakespeare, HAMLET (ca. 1601)
       John Webster, THE DUCHESS OF MALFI (1612–1613)

reversal [rɪˈvɜːsl] (n.): cf. *peripeteia*.

review [rɪˈvjuː] (n.): a short critical evaluation of a work of literature, art, etc. Reviews are usually published in newspapers, *journals* or similar publications. The word "review" is also used to refer to a periodical which contains articles dealing with artistic or technical subjects.

rhapsody [ˈræpsədɪ] (n.): an unrestrained outpouring of thought or feeling.

rhetoric [ˈretərɪk] (n.): the art of using language effectively, either in writing or in speaking, for the purpose of persuasion. In Classical times and during the Renaissance rhetoric was an important field of study. Rhetoric may also be used to describe eloquent, elaborate or stylized language.

rhetorical question [rɪˈtɒrɪkl ☆ -ˈtɔːr-]: a question to which the answer is obvious and therefore not expected. It forces the reader or listener to a certain conclusion and therefore influences his or her thoughts; as such, it is often used in a series in order to heighten the emotional feeling (especially when used at a political meeting, etc.) or as a device for examining motives.

Example: "SHYLOCK: [...] Hath not a Jew
eyes? Hath not a Jew hands,
organs, dimensions, senses,
affections, passions? Fed
with the same food, hurt
with the same weapons,
subject to the same diseases,
healed by the same means,
warmed and cooled by the
same winter and summer, as
a Christian is? If you prick
us, do we not bleed? if you
tickle us, do we not laugh? if
you poison us, do we not die? and if you wrong us, shall we not
revenge?"
(William Shakespeare, THE MERCHANT OF VENICE, III, i, 57–65;
ca. 1596)

rhyme [raɪm] (n.): the likeness of sounds in two or more words extending from the stressed syllable to the end of the word(s). Rhyme is used to achieve a pleasant sound and to underline the structure through *repetition*.
There are various kinds of rhyme:
a) *end rhyme*, where the two rhymes are at the end of a *poem*'s *lines*;
b) *internal rhyme*, where the rhymes are to be found in the middle of a poem's lines;
c) *masculine rhyme*, where the rhyme extends over one syllable;
d) *feminine rhyme*, where the rhyme extends over two or more syllables;
e) *identical rhyme*, where the rhyming words are the same;
f) *pure* (or perfect) rhyme, where the rhyming sounds are exactly the same;
g) *eye-rhyme*, where the words look as though they rhyme because their spellings are alike, but which are in fact pronounced quite differently;
h) *imperfect rhyme*, where the sounds are similar but not exact.

rhyme scheme ['raɪm ˌskiːm]: the arrangement of *rhymes* in a *poem*. It refers to rhymes at the end of the poem's *lines*; the rhymes are indicated by small letters of the alphabet, e.g. a b b a c c , which indicates that the 1st and 4th lines rhyme as do the 2nd and 3rd, and the 5th and 6th; cf. *alternate rhyme*, *enclosed rhyme*.

rhythm ['rɪðəm] (n.), **rhythmic** ['rɪðmɪk] (adj.): the arrangement of stressed or unstressed syllables in writing to produce a certain flow of sound. In *verse*, there is a regular rhythm, usually based around a *metrical* pattern; in *prose*, the rhythm changes according to the sentence and mood.

rising action [,– – '– –]: a structural element of a *fictional* text, marked by an increase in the *suspense* and the intensification of the *conflict*. Rising action usually follows the *exposition* and precedes the *climax*; cf. *plot*.

romantic irony [rǝʊ'mæntɪk]: the interruption of a *narrative* by an *author* to comment on the *characters*, the *plot* or his or her problems as a writer. This is done with the intention of destroying the illusion of reality in a *fictional* text, so that the reader does not take the story too seriously.

Romanticism [rǝʊ'mæntɪsɪzm]: a term used to describe a movement in art and literature which laid emphasis on individual experience, imagination, emotion and the assertion of the self. Landscape and nature were important topics in romantic literature, since, through the appreciation of the harmonious relationships within Nature, humanity was supposed to be able to understand its own behaviour and relationships. The movement lasted from about 1780 until 1830, and is often seen as a reaction against the rationalism of *Classicism*.

round character: a term coined by E.M. Forster in ASPECTS OF THE NOVEL (1927) to describe a *character* in a *fictional* text who develops in the course of the text, and therefore changes his or her attitudes and values; cf. *flat character*.

run-on line [,– – '–]: cf. *enjambement*.

S

sarcasm ['sɑːkæzm] (n.), **sarcastic** [sɑːˈkæstɪk] (adj.): a bitter or aggressive remark used to express mockery or disapproval. It is normally achieved through the use of statements which are the opposite of their *literal* meaning; as such it is a form of *irony*. The dividing line between irony and sarcasm is difficult to distinguish – sarcasm is bitter and overt, irony is gentle and subtle.

satire ['sætaɪə] (n.), **satirical** [səˈtɪrɪkl] (adj.): a *fictional* text intended to criticize certain conditions, events or people by making them appear ridiculous. *Irony* (and *sarcasm*) are important elements in satire. Unlike *comedy*, satire does not seek to produce *humour* and laughter as ends in themselves, rather to use them to deride something. Satire is more often than not used to ridicule some aspect of society.
Example: Jonathan Swift, GULLIVER'S TRAVELS (1726)

scene[1] [siːn] (n.): a subdivision of an *act* of a *play*, usually consisting of unity of time, place and *action*.

scene[2] [siːn] (n.): the place of *action* in a *play* or *narrative* text; cf. *setting*.

scenic presentation [,– – ,– – '– –]: a *mode of presentation* in which the elements and *action* of a story are shown in detail, thus encouraging the reader or listener to participate directly in the action; cf. *panoramic presentation*.

science fiction [,saɪəns ˈfɪkʃən]: a *fictional* text in which scientific developments or discoveries play an important role. Often science fiction stories are set in the future. They may deal with the consequences, beneficial or detrimental, which scientific discoveries have on society; cf. *utopia, anti-utopia*.

sea shanty ['siː ʃæntɪ]: a song sung by sailors while they worked on board a ship. Sea shanties helped coordinate group work, since the *rhythms* of the songs matched the rhythms of the sailors' tasks. It also helped maintain morale. Shanties were popular throughout the 17th, 18th and 19th centuries.
Example: "What shall we do with a drunken sailor?"

septet [sepˈtet] (n.): a *stanza* consisting of seven *lines*.

sermon ['sɜːmən] (n.): a religious discourse, usually delivered as part of a church service.

serpentine verse ['sɜːpəntaɪn ☆ -tiːn]: a *line* of a *poem* which begins and ends with the same word.

sestet [ses'tet] (n.): a *stanza* consisting of six *lines*. A sestet is often the last unit in a Petrarchan *sonnet*, rhyming c d c d c d or c d e e d e. It is also known as a "sixain".

setting ['setɪŋ] (n.): the place and/or time in which an *action* in a text takes place. Example: Ancient Britain is the setting for William Shakespeare's KING LEAR (ca. 1605).

short play: a *drama* which is considerably shorter than a full length play. It normally takes about half an hour to perform and usually observes the *unities*. A short play may have one, two or more *scenes*, episodes or *acts*; cf. *one-act play*.

short short story: a very short story composed of ca. 500 words. Example: Ernest Hemingway, "A Very Short Story" (1924)

short story: a short *fictional narrative* text. It usually consists of a tight *plot*, and is limited in *theme*, *setting* and number of *characters* and events by its length. The short story became popular in the 19th century.
Examples: Edgar Allan Poe, "The Masque of the Red Death" (1841–42)
Katherine Mansfield, "Life of Ma Parker" (1922)
Ernest Hemingway, "Cat in the Rain" (1925)

simile ['sɪmɪlɪ] (n.): an element of *imagery* in which distinctly different things are linked together in the form of an explicit comparison through the words "like" or "as". A simile serves to offer the reader or listener a new insight into the object under discussion; cf. *metaphor*.
Examples: "They argued savagely, nose to nose, in furious whispers which sounded *like the hissing of snakes*."
(Joyce Cary, RED LETTER DAY; 1953)
"O, my love's *like a red, red rose*"
(Robert Burns, "A Red, Red Rose"; ca. 1787)

sixain ['sɪkseɪn]: cf. *sestet*.

sketch[1] [sketʃ] (n.): a short piece of *descriptive* writing, usually about people or places.

sketch[2] [sketʃ] (n.): a short *drama* which is usually *humorous* or thought-provoking, without being profound.

slapstick ['slæpstɪk] (n.): a type of *comedy* which involves *farce* and buffoonery; there is usually a lot of physical action, e.g. hitting, kicking, throwing and falling down.

solecism ['sɒlɪsɪzm ☆ 'sɑːl-] (n.): a deviation from correct syntax or grammar. It is usually found in texts in which slang or dialect are used.
Example: I ain't done nothing.

soliloquy [sə'lɪləkwɪ] (n.): in *drama*, a *speech* delivered by a *character* alone on stage; it is used to reveal a character's thoughts, feelings or motives to the audience. A soliloquy allows the audience to learn more about the character than would be possible if only *action* and *dialogue* were presented; cf. *monologue*.
Example: "HAMLET: To be or not to be; that is the question ..."
(William Shakespeare, HAMLET, III, i, 56–89; ca. 1601)

solution [sə'luːʃn] (n.): cf. *denouement*.

sonnet ['sɒnɪt] (n.): a *poem* consisting of 14 *lines*. English sonnets are usually written in *iambic pentameters*. The sonnet became popular in the 17th century in England and was used mostly for love *poetry*, but later it came to embrace a wide number of *themes*. These are the various types of sonnet:
a) The Italian or Petrarchan sonnet, which comprises an *octave* rhyming a b b a a b b a and a *sestet* rhyming c d e e d e or c d c d c d. In the octave the theme of the sonnet is stated and developed, in the sestet the theme is varied and resolved.
Example: William Wordsworth, "Composed upon Westminster Bridge" (1802)
b) The Spenserian sonnet, which comprises three *quatrains* and a *couplet*; it rhymes a b a b b c b c c d c d e e. The theme develops in each successive quatrain and the resolution is found in the couplet.
c) The Shakespearian sonnet, which comprises three quatrains and a couplet, rhyming a b a b c d c d d e d e g g.
Examples: William Shakespeare's sonnets (1593–1600)

speaker: the *fictional* person, in theory not identical with the poet, who is to be imagined as saying the text of a *poem*, especially a *lyric* poem.

speech [spiːtʃ] (n.): a talk or address delivered to an audience; it is usually written in *formal style*.

spondee ['spɒndiː ☆ 'spɑːn-] (n.), **spondaic** [spɒn'deɪk ☆ spɑːn-] (adj.): a *metrical foot* consisting of two stressed syllables: '– '– . It is only used together with other kinds of feet to give a heavy or melancholy *tone*.

stage directions ['steɪdʒ dəˌrekʃnz]: a playwright's notes in a *drama* which give information about how the drama is to be performed; stage directions may deal with any of the following: *setting*, scenery, *characters'* appearances, movements, tones of speaking and *entrances* and *exits*. They may supply *explicit* as well as *implicit characterization*.

stanza ['stænzə] (n.): a major division in a *poem*; a stanza consists of several *lines* which usually share a particular *rhyme scheme* and *metre* that is repeated in each stanza throughout the poem. It is also called a "verse".

stichomythia [ˌstɪkəʊ'mɪθɪə] (n.): a *dialogue* of alternate single lines, especially in *drama*; it is characterized by the use of *antithesis* and *repetition*, which create *tension* and *conflict*.
Example: "HAMLET: Now, mother, what's the matter?
    QUEEN: Hamlet, thou hast thy father much offended.
    HAMLET: Mother, thou hast my father much offended.
    QUEEN: Come, come, you answer with an idle tongue.
    HAMLET: Go, go, you question with a wicked tongue."
    (William Shakespeare, HAMLET, III, iv, 9–12; ca. 1601)

stock character [ˌ– '– – –]: a *character* who embodies a particular idea or quality and lacks the roundness of a human being. Stock characters are common in literature as backdrops to the main characters. The nagging wife and the bragging soldier are examples of stock characters. Such characters are *archetypal* in that one needs no explanation to recognize them; cf. *flat character*.
Examples: Mistress Overdone in William Shakespeare's MEASURE FOR
    MEASURE (ca. 1604)
    Juliet's nurse in William Shakespeare's ROMEO AND JULIET (ca. 1595)

story of initiation: cf. *coming-of-age story*.

stream of consciousness ['kɒnʃəsnəs ☆ 'kɑːn-]: the presentation of experience through the mind of one *character* in a text. All *action* in the text is then presented from the *point of view* of that character and events are portrayed only in so far as they impinge on the consciousness of that character. *Interior monologue* is one technique used within the stream of consciousness.
Example: "It was unfair and cruel because the doctor had told him not to read without glasses and he had written home to his father that

morning to send him a new pair. And Father Arnall had said that he need not study till the new glasses came. Then to be called a schemer before the whole class ..."
(James Joyce, A PORTRAIT OF THE ARTIST AS A YOUNG MAN; 1916)

style [staɪl] (n.): a writer's way of expressing him or herself. Style involves the method of conveying what the writer wants to say in an effective way. Style comprises the choice of words, the *tone*, *atmosphere*, sentence structure and the *mode of presentation*; cf. *formal style*, *informal style*, *neutral style*.

subplot ['sʌbplɒt ☆ -plɑːt] (n.): in a *fictional* text, a subsidiary *action* which contrasts with or complements the main action.

substance ['sʌbstəns] (n.): the content of a literary text; that which is said, rather than how it is said; cf. *form*.

summary ['sʌmərɪ] (n.): a *text form* belonging to the *text type exposition*; it is a short text presenting the most important information from some other text. A summary does not contain the summary writer's own personal opinions or interpretations. It is also known as a "précis".

surprise ending [– ,– '– –]: a sudden and unexpected turn of fortune or *action* which ends a *narrative* text.

surrealism [sə'rɪəlɪzm] (n.): a movement in art in the 1920s which sought to express the subconscious. Surrealism attempted to discover the hidden psyche through automatic writing, whereby thoughts were written down at random, and through studying dreams.

suspense [sə'spens] (n.): a feeling of *tension* or expectation aroused in the reader or audience about the further development of the *plot* in a *fictional* text.

suspension of disbelief [sə'spenʃn əv ˌdɪsbə'liːf]: the ability of a reader or listener to accept that a work of the imagination is real. This is especially necessary in *drama*, when the audience, in order to become involved, must suspend its disbelief. The term was coined by Samuel Coleridge in BIOGRAPHIA LITERARIA (1817).

syllabic verse [sɪ'læbɪk]: a type of *verse* measured by the number of syllables in each *line* rather than by the stress of the syllables.

syllepsis [sɪ'lepsɪs] (n.): a stylistic device in which one word is applied to two or more other words in different senses. The term *zeugma* is often used instead of syllepsis, although strictly speaking it has a slightly different meaning.

Examples: "He felt perfectly capable of being in disgrace and in a gooseberry
garden at the same moment."
(Saki, "The Lumber-Room"; ca. 1905)
"Miss Bolo ... went straight home in a flood of tears and a sedan
chair."
(Charles Dickens, THE PICKWICK PAPERS; 1837)

symbol ['sɪmbl] (n.), **symbolic(al)** [sɪm'bɒlɪk(l) ☆ -'bɑːl-] (adj.): an element of
imagery, in which a concrete object stands not only for itself but for some
abstract idea as well. Symbols are an important element in all literature.
Examples: A red rose can be a symbol of love or beauty.
A pomegranate may stand for the soul, virginity, sexuality or
stupidity.

syncope ['sɪŋkəpɪ] (n.): the omission of sounds or letters in the middle of words.
Syncope may be used to indicate dialect or slang being used in a text or to
accommodate the *metre* in a *poem*.
Examples: o'er (for "over"); e'er (for "ever")

synecdoche [sɪ'nekdəkɪ] (n.): a stylistic device in which a part stands for the
whole of something, or vice versa; cf. *metonomy*.
Examples: "Daily bread" stands for food or meals.
"A hired hand" stands for a person who has been employed on a
temporary basis.
"Jack Lawton's yellow boots dodged out the ball and all the other
boots and *legs* ran after."
(James Joyce, A PORTRAIT OF THE ARTIST AS A YOUNG MAN;
1916)

synthesis ['sɪnθəsɪs]: cf. *dialectical order*.

T

tale [teɪl]: a short *narrative* text. Tales are more closely related to oral literary tradition than other short narrative texts, such as *short stories*.

tall tale/story: a story which is extravagant and either for the most part untrue or greatly exaggerated. Many tall tales developed in the "frontier" lands of the USA.
Example: Mark Twain, "The Jumping Frog of Calaveras County" (1865)

tautology [tɔː'tɒlədʒɪ ☆ -'taːl-] (n.),
    tautological [tɔːtə'lɒdʒɪkl ☆ -'laːdʒ-] (adj.): the use of more words than is necessary; cf. *pleonasm*.
Examples: (To) hear with one's ears; Personally speaking, I myself would ...; At this moment in time

technical description ['teknɪkl]: the presentation of the physical characteristics of living beings, objects or processes based on the writer's exact observations in order to provide objective information; cf. *impressionistic description*.

telling name ['– – –]: in a *narrative* text, a person's name which reveals one or more of his or her characteristic traits.
Examples: Wackford Squeers in Charles Dickens's Nicholas Nickleby (1838–1839) – his weird and tyrannical nature are indicated by "wack" and "queer" which make up his name.
Stephen Dedalus in James Joyce's A Portrait of the Artist as a Young Man (1916) – Stephen refers to the first Christian martyr and Dedalus refers to an artist and genius who lived in ancient Greece.

temporal order ['tempərəl]: the structuring of a text by presenting actions and events in relation to time. The most common type of temporal order is *chronological order*.

tension ['tenʃn] (n.): the emotional strain in a text caused by the *conflict* of opposing forces.

tercet ['tɜːsɪt] (n.): a *stanza* of three *lines*, or half of the *sestet* in a *sonnet*.

tetralogy [təˈtrælədʒɪ] (n.): a set of four pieces of literary work, connected with one another in some way, e.g. by *theme* and/or *characters*.
Example: The War of the Roses tetralogy by William Shakespeare
(HENRY VI, Parts I, II and III; ca. 1590; and RICHARD III; ca. 1594)

tetrameter [teˈtræmɪtə] (n.): a *line* of four *metrical* feet (cf. *foot*); it usually consists of *iambs* [– ʹ–] or *trochees* [ʹ– –].

text form: the classification of a text according to the form in which it is presented, e.g. as a *poem*, a *short story*, a *novel*, a *report*.

text type: the classification of the text according to the writer's intentions. There are five different models of text types: *argumentation*, *description*, *exposition*, *instruction*, *narration*. Though most texts contain elements of several text types, one is usually dominant.

theatre of the absurd ☆ **theater** [əbˈsɜːd]: a term applied to a category of *drama* in which the rules of formal logic and conventional structure are ignored. Human beings are revealed as struggling to survive in a destructive and irrational world, where cause and effect no longer exist. Theatre of the absurd developed in the 1950s and was influenced by *Existentialism*.
Example: Samuel Beckett, WAITING FOR GODOT (1955).

theme [θiːm] (n.): the central topic or idea in a text which binds all its elements together.
Example: The theme of William Shakespeare's OTHELLO (ca. 1604) is jealousy.

thesis [ˈθiːsɪs]: cf. *dialectical order*.

third-person narrator: a *narrator* who stands outside the story and uses the third person voice ("he", "she" or "they") to refer to the *characters*. A third person narrator may tell the story as an *omniscient narrator* with an *unlimited point of view* or from the point of view of one of the characters. This latter technique led to the development of the *stream of consciousness* method of *narration*.

tone [təʊn] (n.): the writer's or speaker's attitude towards his or her *theme*, *characters*, or readers/listeners. The tone in a text can be, for example, serious or playful, *humorous* or solemn, *ironical* or romantic; cf. *atmosphere*.

topical order ['tɒpɪkl ☆ 'tɑːp-]: the structuring of a text according to its main topics, following logical steps and categories.

topos ['tɒpɒs], pl. **topoi** ['tɒpɔɪ]: a *theme* or *motif* which recurs throughout literature.
Examples: the aubade (the parting of lovers at dawn)
the *carpe diem* (the enjoyment of each day to its fullest)
the ubi sunt (a *lament* on the transitory nature of life)

tract [trækt] (n.): a short *pamphlet*, usually dealing with a political or religious subject.

tragedy ['trædʒədɪ] (n.), **tragic** ['– –] (adj.): a form of *drama* in which the *protagonist* passes through a series of misfortunes towards his or her downfall. According to Aristotle, tragedy centres around a tragic *hero* who because of his or her *hamartia* (tragic flaw) suffers a reversal of fortune (cf. *perepeteia*) from happiness to misery. Although his definition of tragedy was influential in English drama, it was Seneca's emphasis on revenge, murder and carnage that proved more popular to *Elizabethan* dramatists. The protagonist may be good or evil, but the tragedy that befalls him or her is usually partly of his or her own making.
Examples: William Shakespeare, MACBETH (ca. 1606) and OTHELLO (ca. 1604)
Arthur Miller, DEATH OF A SALESMAN (1949)

tragic flaw: cf. *hamartia*.

tragic irony: *dramatic irony* which is used in tragedies. The audience knows more than the *characters* do.
Example: In William Shakespeare's ROMEO AND JULIET (ca. 1595) Romeo kills himself when he discovers Juliet's seemingly lifeless body. However, as the audience knows, Juliet has only taken a potion to make her appear dead.

tragicomedy [ˌtrædʒɪ'kɒmədɪ ☆ -'kɑːm-] (n.): a *drama* in which there are elements of *tragedy* and *comedy*. In the Renaissance tragicomedies were marked by the inclusion of *characters* of high and low birth. Although a tragicomedy has a happy or at least a non-tragic ending, it is overshadowed by the more sombre events that occur in the *play*.
Examples: William Shakespeare, THE MERCHANT OF VENICE (ca.1596)
Samuel Beckett, WAITING FOR GODOT (1955)

Transcendentalism: a movement centred in New England in the 1830s and 40s that held that basic truths can be understood through intuition rather than through reason. As such the movement had its roots in *Romanticism*. The Transcendentalists believed that people should live in harmony with nature and as simply as possible. Among its proponents were Ralph Waldo Emerson and Henry David Thoreau.

treatise ['triːtɪz ☆ -əs] (n.): a *non-fictional text form* consisting of a careful examination of one particular subject.
Example: David Hume, TREATISE OF HUMAN NATURE (1739–1740)

trilogy ['trɪlədʒɪ] (n.): a set of three pieces of literary work connected with one another in some way, especially by *theme* and/or *characters*.

trimeter ['trɪmɪtə] (n.): a *line* of three *metrical* feet (cf. *foot*).

trochee ['trəʊkiː] (n.), **trochaic** [trəʊ'keɪk] (adj.): a *metrical foot* consisting of an initial stressed syllable followed by an unstressed one: '– – . It is usually used in combination with other feet. If used as the predominant foot, the last syllable in the *line* is normally stressed.
Example: "Tíger,| Tíger,| búrning | bríght
Ín the | fórest | óf the | níght"
(William Blake, "The Tiger"; 1794)

turning point ['– – –]: a structural element of a *fictional* text, marking a change in the *conflict* or *suspense*. It usually follows the *climax* and precedes the *falling action*. Turning point and *crisis* are often the same in *tragedy*; cf. *plot*.

type [taɪp]: a *character* in a *fictional* text who is not fully developed, but is one-sided and represents a group of people or some human trait rather than an individual.

U

understatement [ˌʌndə'steɪtmənt] (n.): a statement that is deliberately weak, putting less emphasis or importance on something than it deserves; understatement is often used for ironical effect. It differs from *litotes* in that it understates something, while litotes usually through the negative of something expresses the affirmative.
Example: "The reports of my death are greatly exaggerated."
(Mark Twain; ca. 1890)

unities, the ['juːnɪtiːz]: the three principles of dramatic composition: unity of *action*, time and place. These unities require that the action of a *drama* should be unified, i.e. be without distracting *subplots*, that the action should last no longer than 24 hours and should be confined to one place. The unities derive from Aristotle and played an important role in European Renaissance drama; English dramatists, however, have rarely used the three unities in their *plays*.

unlimited point of view: the use of a non-personal *narration*, in which all aspects of the *characters'* personalities, histories and actions may be examined. An unlimited point of view is used by an *omniscient narrator*.

utopia [juː'təʊpɪə] (n.), **utopian** [– '– –] (adj.): a *fictional* text dealing with an ideal society or world. The idea of a utopian society is of great antiquity, being found in the Bible and the works of Homer and Plato. The term derives from Thomas More's UTOPIA (1516). In modern literature the *anti-utopian novel* has become more popular than the utopian.

V

verse[1] [vɜːs] (n.): a term used to describe *poetry*, especially if written in *metre*. Verse is often used to describe light-hearted poems; cf. *blank verse, free verse, narrative verse, nonsense verse, syllabic verse.*

verse[2] [vɜːs] (n.): a *stanza* in a *poem* or song.

Victorian [vɪk'tɔːrɪən] (adj.): referring to the reign of Queen Victoria (1837–1901). This era was characterized by strict morality and adherence to orthodoxy, but also by radical social change. *Poetry* and *novel*-writing flourished, but little of note was produced in *drama*. Among the writers belonging to this era are Charles Dickens, the Brontë sisters, Thomas Hardy and the Brownings.

view point: cf. *point of view.*

villain ['vɪlən] (n.): the bad *character* in any *fictional* text who contrives to destroy the *hero* or heroine.
Example: Iago in William Shakespeare's OTHELLO (ca. 1604).

villanelle [ˌvɪlə'nel] (n.): a type of *poem* consisting of five *tercets* rhyming a b a and a final *quatrain* rhyming a b a a. The first and third *lines* of the first tercet are repeated alternately throughout the poem, and together form the last two lines of the quatrain. Villanelles were originally used in the 16th century in pastoral *poetry*.
Example: Dylan Thomas, "Do Not Go Gentle into that Good Night" (1946)

Z

zeugma ['zjuːgmə ☆ 'zuːg-] (n.): a stylistic device that relates one word to two or more words, when it is only appropriate to one of the words. Zeugma and *syllepsis*, however, are often used interchangeably, although strictly speaking their meanings are slightly different: in a syllepsis the single word makes sense with both of the other words.

Example: "See Pan *with* flocks, *with* fruits Pomona *crowned*."
(Alexander Pope, "Windsor Forest"; 1713)
Here "crowned" applies correctly only to "with fruits".

List of Literary Terms in Wordfields

plot
exposition[1]
rising action
climax
crisis
turning point
falling action
catastrophe
denouement
solution
open ending
surprise ending

action
conflict
  external conflict
  internal conflict
suspense
tension

anticipation
foreshadowing
flashback
subplot
frame story

narration
point of view
viewpoint
  unlimited point of view
  limited point of view
narrator
  omniscient narrator
  third-person narrator
  first-person narrator
  intrusive narrator
  dramatized narrator
stream of consciousness
interior monologue

mode of presentation
panoramic presentation
scenic presentation
narrating time
acting time
reading time

poetry
verse[1]
poem

speaker
poetic diction

acrostic
ballad
carol
concrete poem
elegy
epic
idyll
limerick
lyric
mock epic
narrative verse
nursery rhyme
nonsense verse
ode
pattern poem
sea shanty
sonnet
villanelle

stanza
  tercet
  quatrain
  quintain
  quintet
  sestet
  sixain
  septet
  octet
  octave
verse[2]
chorus[2]
canto
refrain
envoy

rhythm
metre
  trimeter
  tetrameter
  pentameter
  hexameter

foot
  anapaest
  dactyl
  iamb
  spondee
  trochee

counterpoint
anacrusis

alexandrine
blank verse
free verse
heroic couplet
serpentine verse
syllabic verse

rhyme
  end rhyme
  internal rhyme
  identical rhyme
  perfect rhyme
  pure rhyme
  eye rhyme
  imperfect rhyme
  feminine rhyme
  masculine rhyme
rhyme scheme
  alternate rhyme
  enclosed rhyme
  couplet

line
  end-stopped line
  enjambement
  run-on-line
caesura

drama
play
act
scene[1]
setting
scene[2]
unities

comedy
tragedy
tragicomedy
melodrama
burlesque
farce
low comedy
slapstick
sketch[2]
revenge tragedy
kitchen-sink drama

81

comedy of manners
Restoration comedy
pantomime

monodrama
one-act play
short play

comic relief
interlude

aside
monologue
soliloquy
stichomythia
dialogue
duologue

catharsis
alienation effect
estrangement
suspension of disbelief

hamartia
tragic flaw
hubris
anagnorisis
peripeteia
reversal
recoil
tragic irony
dramatic irony
poetic justice

stage directions
entrance
exit

character
protagonist
hero/heroine
antagonist
villain
anti-hero
foil
chorus[1]

archetype
type
stock character
flat character
round character
caricature
telling name

delineation
characterization
    direct characterization
    explicit characterization
    indirect characterization
    implicit characterization

order
chronological order
climactic order
contrastive order
dialectical order
    thesis
    antithesis[2]
    synthesis
listing order
temporal order
topical order

text type
argumentation
description
exposition
instruction
narration

text form
poem
drama
novel
novella
novelette
anti-novel
short story
short short story
prose poem
fairy tale
fable
parable
anecdote
epigram
aphorism
adage
proverb
repartee

report
interpretive news story
news story
feature story
editorial
leader
leading article
letter to the editor

interview
review

comment
essay
sermon
tract
treatise

memoirs
autobiography
biography
journal
diary

abstract
summary
outline
keyword outline
paraphrase
précis

rhetorical devices
accumulation
alliteration
allegory
amplification
anacoluthon
anaphora
allusion
antiphrasis
antithesis[1]
apostrophe
argumentum ad hominem
assonance
bathos
cacophony
carpe diem
catachresis
chiasmus
cliché
conceit
consonance
dead metaphor
deus ex machina
ellipsis
epithet
euphemism
euphony
euphuism
exaggeration
hendiadys
hyberbole
image

82

irony
leitmotif
litotes
malapropism
meiosis
metaphor
metonomy
mixed metaphor
motif
onomatopoeia
oxymoron
paradox
parallelism
pathetic fallacy
periphrasis
personification
pleonasm
pun
repetition
rhapsody
rhetorical question
sarcasm
simile
solecism
syllepsis
symbol
syncope
synecdoche
tautology
topos
understatement
zeugma

German-English Index

There will undoubtedly be occasions when you know a particular term in German but not in English. The German-English Index will help you find the English term. You should always check on the definition in the glossary under the English headword just to make sure that it corresponds to what you think the German term means.

Because the history of literary theory in the English- and German-speaking worlds is not identical, you will discover that most terms are not exact equivalents. In the index the similarities and differences between the terms have been pointed out. The symbol "=" means that the terms are identical or very close; "–" means that the terms are close in meaning or that both terms have several meanings, some of which are not covered by the term in the other language; ">" means that the German term has a wider field of application than the English term; "<" means that the German term has a narrower field of application than the English term; "≠" means that the terms are false friends, i.e. that they look as though they ought to mean the same in both languages, but that their meanings are in fact quite different.

Abgang = exit
Abhandlung – treatise
Abriß – outline
Abschweifung – digression
Absurdes Theater = theatre
  (☆ theater) of the absurd
Achtzeiler = octave, octet
Akkumulation =
  accumulation
Akrostichon = acrostic
Akt = act
Alexandriner = alexandrine
Allegorie = allegory
allegorisch = allegorical
Alliteration = alliteration
alliterieren = alliterate
allwissender Erzähler =
  omniscient narrator
Ambiguität = ambiguity
Amplifikatio(n) =
  amplification
Anagnorisis = anagnorisis
Anakoluth = anacoluthon
Anakrusis = anacrusis
Anapäst = anapaest
anapästisch = anapaestic
Anapher = anaphora
Anaphora = anaphora
Anekdote = anecdote
Anrede – apostrophe
Anspielung = allusion

Antagonist/in = antagonist
Antiheld = anti-hero
Antiklimax = anti-climax
Antiphrase = antiphrasis
Antiroman = anti-novel
Antithese = antithesis[1+2]
antithetisch = antithetic(al)
Anti-Utopie = anti-utopia
Antizipation = anticipation
à part = aside
Aparte = aside
Aphorismus = aphorism
aphoristisch = aphoristic
apokalyptische Literatur =
  apocalyptic literature
apologetisch = apologetic
Apologie = apology
Apostroph = apostrophe
Archetyp(us) = archetype
archetypisch = archetypal
Argumentation =
  argumentation
Assonanz < assonance
Atmosphäre = atmosphere
Aufbau – order
Aufklärung =
  Enlightenment
Aufsatz = essay
Auftakt = anacrusis
Auftritt[1] > scene
Auftritt[2] = entrance

Aufzug = act
Augenreim = eye-rhyme
auktorialer Erzähler =
  omniscient narrator
Ausgang = denouement
ausgleichende
  Gerechtigkeit = poetic
  justice
Auslassung > ellipsis
Außenperspektive =
  unlimited point of view
äußerer Konflikt = external
  conflict
Autobiographie =
  autobiography
autobiographisch =
  autobiographical
Autor/in = author
Avantgarde = avant garde

Ballade > ballad
Bänkellied – ballad
bathetisch = bathetic
Bathos = bathos
Bedeutung = denotation
Beiseite-Gespräch = aside
Beiseitesprechen = aside
belehrend – instructive
Belehrung – instruction
Belletristik – fiction
belletristisch – fictional

Bericht = report
berichtende Erzählung =
    panoramic presentation
Beschimpfung – invective
beschreibend = descriptive
Beschreibung = description
Bewußtseinsstrom =
    stream of consciousness
Bild = image
Bildbruch/-vermengung =
    mixed metaphor;
    – catachresis
bilderreich/bildlich <
    figurative
Bildersprache = imagery
Binnenreim = internal
    rhyme
Biographie = biography
biographisch =
    biographical
Blankvers = blank verse
Bösewicht = villain
Broschüre < pamphlet
Buchbesprechung < review
Bühnenanweisungen =
    stage directions
Burleske = burlesque

Charakter < Character;
    – round character
charakterisieren =
    characterize
Charakterisierung =
    characterization
Charakterzeichnung =
    characterization
Chiasmus = chiasmus
Chor > chorus

daktylisch = dactylic
Daktylus = dactyl
Denotation = denotation
Dénouement =
    denouement
derbe Komödie – low
    comedy
Deus ex machina = deus ex
    machina
Dialog = dialogue
Diatribe ≠ diatribe
dichterische Sprache =
    poetic diction
didaktisch = didactic

direkte Charakterisierung
    = direct/explicit charac-
    terization
Dokument = document
Dokumentarliteratur/-
    roman – faction
doppeldeutig = ambiguous
Doppeldeutigkeit =
    ambiguity
Drama = drama
dramatische Ironie =
    dramatic irony
Dreiheber = trimeter
Dreizeiler = tercet
Dystopie = dystopia

Einakter = one-act play
Einfühlung(svermögen) =
    empathy
Einheiten = unities
Elegie = elegy
elisabethanisch =
    Elizabethan
Ellipse = ellipsis
Eloge = eulogy
Empirizismus = empiricism
Endreim = end rhyme
Enjambement =
    enjambement
Entspannungskomik –
    comic relief
Envoi = envoy
Epigramm = epigram
Epigraph = epigraph
Epilog = epilogue
episch = epic
Episode = episode
Epitaph = epitaph
Epitheton = epithet
Epos = epic
Er-Erzähler = third-person
    narrator
Erkennung > anagnorisis
erlebte Rede = stream of
    consciousness
Erwiderung (geistreiche) –
    repartee
Erzählen = narration,
    narrative
Erzähler/in = narrator
Erzählerstandpunkt –
    point of view, viewpoint
Erzählgedicht/-lied –
    ballad

Erzählperspektive/-winkel
    – point of view,
    viewpoint
erzählte Zeit = acting time
Erzählung > narration,
    narrative, tale
Erzählzeit = narrating time
Essay = essay
Euphemismus =
    euphemism
euphemistisch =
    euphemistic
Euphonie = euphony
Euphuismus = euphuism
Existentialismus =
    Existentialism
Exposition = exposition[1+2]
Expressionismus =
    Expressionism
Extrapolation =
    extrapolation
Extrapolierung =
    extrapolation

Fabel = fable
Fachliteratur < non-fiction
Fachprosa < non-fiction
familiär – informal
fallende Handlung = falling
    action
Farce = farce
Feature > feature story
Figur < character
figurengebundene Erzähl-
    perspektive = limited
    point of view
figürlich < figurative
Fiktion = fiction
fiktional/fiktiv = fictional
fiktiv – fictitious
Flugschrift < pamphlet
Form = form
formell = formal
Fragepronomen – five w's
freie Rhythmen = free verse
freie Verse ≠ free verse
Fünfheber – pentameter
Fünfzeiler = quintain,
    quintet
Fuß = foot

Gattung – genre
Gebrauchsmetapher –
    dead metaphor

85

Gedicht = poem
Gegenspieler/in = antagonist
Gehalt – substance
gehobener Stil – formal style
Gemeinplatz – cliché
Genre – genre, text form
Gesang > canto
Geschichte > tale
Gestalt – form
Gleichnis – parable
Gleichnis > simile
Grabschrift = epitaph
grotesk = grotesque
Groteske = grotesque
Grundform des Erzählens = mode of presentation

Hamartia = hamartia
Handlung – plot
Handlung(sverlauf) – action
Handlungsabfall = falling action
Handlungsanstieg = rising action
Handlungsraum – setting
Häufung = accumulation
Hauptfigur = protagonist
Held = hero
Heldin = heroine
Hendiadys/-dyion = hendiadys
Hexameter < hexameter
Höhepunkt = climax
Homophon = homophone
Humor = humour (☆ humor)
Hybris = hubris
Hyperbel = hyperbole

Ich-Erzähler/in = first-person narrator
identischer Reim = identical rhyme
Idyll(e) = idyll
idyllisch = idyllic
Imagismus = Imagism
indirekte Charakterisierung = indirect/implicit characterization
informell = informal

Inhalt – substance
Innenperspektive = limited point of view
innerer Konflikt = internal conflict
innerer Monolog = interior monologue
intensivierendes Adverb = intensifying adverb
Interludium/-lude = interlude
Interview = interview
Invektive = invective
Ironie = irony
ironisch = ironic

jambisch = iambic
Jambus = iamb
Journal = journal

Kakophonie = cacophony
Kalauer – pun
Karikatur > caricature; > cartoon
Katachrese = catachresis
Katastrophe = catastrophe
Katharsis = catharsis
Kehrreim = refrain
Kinderlied/-vers – nursery rhyme
Kitschroman < novelette
Klage(lied/-gedicht) – lament, elegy
Klangmalerei = onomatopoeia
Klassizismus < classicism
Klimax = climax
klingender Reim = feminine rhyme
Klischee = cliché
komisch = comic
komische Entspannung = comic relief
komisches Epos = mock epic
Kommentar – comment
Konflikt = conflict
konkrete Poesie = concrete poetry
Konnotation = connotation
Konspekt – précis
Kontrast = contrast
Kontrastfigur > foil

kontrastierend/kontrastiv = contrastive
Konversationsstück – comedy of manners
Konzetto = conceit
Kreuzreim = alternate rhyme
Krisis = crisis
Kritik > review
Kurzgeschichte = short story
Kurzroman – novella

langes Reimpaar – heroic couplet
Lautmalerei = onomatopoeia
lautmalerisch = onomatopoeic/-poetic
Lautung – onomatopoeia
Lautsymbolik – onomatopoeia
Layout = layout
Legende = legend
Leitartikel = editorial, leader, leading article
Leitmotiv = leitmotif
Leserbrief – letter to the editor
Lesezeit = reading time
Limerick = limerick
Litotes = litotes
Lobgedicht/-rede – eulogy
Lokalkolorit = local colour/color
Lösung (des Konfliktes) = denouement, solution
Lügenmärchen/-dichtung – tall tale/story
Lyrik – lyric; – poem
lyrisch = lyrical
lyrisches Ich/Subjekt – speaker

männlicher Reim = masculine rhyme
Märchen = fairy tale; – tale
Matrosenlied – sea shanty
mehrdeutig < ambiguous
Mehrdeutigkeit < ambiguity
Meiosis = meiosis
Melodrama > melodrama
Memoiren = memoirs

Metapher = metaphor
metaphorisch =
metaphorical
Metonymie = metonymy
Metrum = metre(☆ meter)
Milieu – setting
Mißklang = cacophony
Monodrama = monodrama
Monolog = monologue;
> soliloquy
Moral = moral
Motiv = motif
Motto > epigraph
Münchhaus(en)iade – tall
tale/story
Mythe/Mythos = myth
mythisch = mythical

Nachrichten(meldung) –
news story
Naturalismus = naturalism
Nebenhandlung = subplot
negative/r Held/in < anti-
hero
Neuklassik ≠
Neoclassicism
neutraler Stil = neutral
style
nicht fiktional/fiktiv =
non-fictional
Nonsensdichtung =
nonsense verse
Novelle = novella

Ode = ode
offener Schluß = open
ending
offene Zeile =
enjambement
onomatopoetisch =
onomatopoeic/-poetic
Onomatopoiesis/-pöie =
onomatopoeia
Ort der Handlung = scene²
Ortskolorit – local color
Oxymoron = oxymoron

Palindrom = palindrome
Pamphlet < pamphlet
Panegyrikus/-kos =
panegyric, eulogy
Parabel = parable
Paradox(on) = paradox
Parallelismus = parallelism

Paraphrase = paraphrase
Parodie = parody
Pathos = pathos
Pausazeile = end-stopped
line
Pentameter < pentameter
Peripetie = perpeteia,
peripety, reversal
Periphrase = periphrasis
personale/r Erzähler/in –
dramatized narrator
Personenverzeichnis >
dramatis personae
Personifikation =
personification
persönliche/r Erzähler/in –
dramatized narrator
Perspektive = point of view
Phrase – cliché
Plagiat = plagiarism
Pleonasmus = pleonasm
pleonastisch = pleonastic
Poeta laureatus = poet
laureate
poetische Diktion = poetic
diction
poetische Gerechtigkeit =
poetic justice
Posse – farce, slapstick
Predigt = sermon
Prosa = prose
Prosagedicht = prose poem
Protagonist/in =
protagonist

Quatrain = quatrain

Rachetragödie = revenge
tragedy
Rahmenerzählung = frame
story
Realismus = realism
Rede = speech
Refrain = refrain
Regieanweisungen = stage
directions
Reihenfolge = order
Reim = rhyme
Reimpaar = couplet
Reimschema = rhyme
scheme
reiner Reim = perfect/pure
rhyme
Rezension > review

Rhapsodie = rhapsody
Rhetorik = rhetoric
rhetorische Frage =
rhetorical question
rhythmisch = rhythmic
Rhythmus = rhythm
Roman > novel
Romantik = Romanticism
romantische Ironie =
romantic irony
Rückblende = flashback
runde Figur = round
character

Sachliteratur = non-fiction
Sage < legend, tale
Sarkasmus = sarcasm
sarkastisch = sarcastic
Satire = satire
satirisch – satirical
Satzbruch = anacoluthon
Schauer(-roman, usw.) =
Gothic
Schauplatz = scene²;
– setting
Schauspiel – drama; < play
schildern = delineate
Schilderung = delineation
Schlußstrophe > envoy
Schmähschrift/-rede >
diatribe; – invective
Schriftstück – document
Schurke/in = villain
Schwank > farce, low
comedy, slapstick
schwarze Komödie = black
comedy
schwarzer Humor = black
humour (☆ humor)
Schwulst – euphuism
Science-fiction = science
fiction
Sechsheber = hexameter
Sechszeiler = sestet, sixain
Seemannslied – sea shanty
Seitengestaltung – layout
Selbstgespräch – soliloquy
Shanty = sea shanty
siebenzeilige Strophe =
septet
silbenzählende Verse =
syllabic verse
Sinnbild > symbol
Sinngedicht = epigram

Sittenkomödie/-stück = comedy of manners
Sketch = sketch[2]
Skizze = sketch[1]
Soliloquium = soliloquy
Solözismus = solecism
Sonett = sonnet
Spannung = suspense, tension
Spondeus = spondee
spondeisch = spondaic
sprechender Name = telling name
Sprichwort = proverb
Stabreim = alliteration
Stanze ≠ stanza
Steigerung = gradation
zeitliche Reihenfolge = chronological order
Stichomythie = stichomythia
Stil = style
Stimmung – atmosphere
Strophe – stanza, verse
stumpfer Reim = masculine rhyme
Stück (Theater-) = play
Substanz = substance
Surrealismus = surrealism
Syllepse = syllepsis
Symbol = symbol
symbolisch = symbolic
Synekdoche = synechdoche
Synkope = syncope
Synthese = synthesis
Szene = scene[1]
szenische Anmerkungen/ Anweisungen = stage directions
szenische Darstellung = scenic presentation

Tagebuch = diary
Tanzlied – carol
Tatsachenliteratur/-roman – faction
Tautologie = tautology
Tenor – tone
Terzett < tercet
Tetralogie = tetralogy
Tetrameter = tetrameter
Textsorte = text form

Texttyp = text type
Theater des Absurden = theatre (☆ theater) of the absurd
Theaterstück = play
Thema = theme
These = thesis
Topos = topos
Tragikomödie = tragicomedy
tragische Ironie = tragic irony
tragischer Fehler = hamartia
Tragödie = tragedy
Traktat = tract
Trauerspiel – tragedy
Trilogie = trilogy
Trimeter ≠ trimeter
Trochäus = trochee
trochäisch = trochaic
Typ – flat character; < type

überraschender Schluß = surprise ending
übertragen < figurative
Übertreibung = exaggeration, hyperbole
umarmender Reim = enclosed rhyme
umschließender Reim = enclosed rhyme
Umschreibung = paraphrase; – periphrasis
Umschwung der Handlung = turning point
ungezwungen – informal
unpersönliche/r Erzähler/in = disguised narrator
unreiner Reim = imperfect rhyme
Untertreibung – litotes; – meiosis; = understatement
Utopie – utopia
utopisch – utopian

Verfasser/in – author
Verfremdung < estrangement
Verfremdungseffekt = alienation effect

Vergleich = simile
Vers < line
Vers(e) < verse
Verserzählung – narrative verse
Versfuß = foot
Versmaß = metre
verstärkendes Adverb = intensifying adverb
Verteidigungsschrift – apology
Vierheber = tetrameter
Viertakter = tetrameter
Vierzeiler = quatrain
viktorianisch = Victorian
Villanelle = villanelle
Vorgriff – anticipation, foreshadowing
Vorwegnahme – anticipation, foreshadowing

weiblicher Reim = feminine rhyme
Weihnachtslied < carol
Weiterdenken = extrapolation
Wendepunkt = turning point; – crisis,
Wiederholung = repetition
Wohlklang = euphony
Wortspiel > pun

Zäsur = caesura
Zeile = line
Zeilenrede – stichomythia
Zeilensprung = enjambement
Zeitschrift – journal; > review
Zeugma = zeugma
Zusammenfassung – précis; = summary
zweideutig < ambiguous
Zweideutigkeit < ambiguity
Zweizeiler = couplet
Zwiegespräch – duologue
Zwischenspiel = interlude
zynisch = cynical
Zynismus = cynicism